Berkley/Reader's Digest books

THE EDITORS OF *READER'S DIGEST*

SUPER WORD POWER

A BERKLEY/READER'S DIGEST BOOK
published by
BERKLEY BOOKS, NEW YORK

SUPER WORD POWER

A Berkley / Reader's Digest Book, published by arrangement with Reader's Digest Press

PRINTING HISTORY
Berkley / Reader's Digest edition / August 1982

Cover design by Sam Salant.

ISBN: 0-425-05609-0

Contents

INTRODUCTION

A New Age
of Words

By PETER FUNK

Our electronic age has given rise to an explosion in language that has had a direct effect on all of us: Thanks to the multitude of new and improved forms of communication, we are being showered with words.

To give some perspective to what's happening, Shakespeare had about 100,000 words to choose from as he wrote his plays and sonnets. *You* have a million and more—ten times his number! But who can deal with so many words, with more being added each day?

You'd think this number would be bad enough. It's not. Our language is as restless as the sea. Old words die off. Others acquire additional meanings. And it's becoming speedier. The tendency is for older words to become shorter, visually more to the point. The luscious, lollygagging, sesquipedalian words of the past are being stripped down and simplified for action.

The English language has never been on a leash. It has been free to roam and pick and bring home friends from all over the world. These new words are coming into your life from science, technology, ethnic groups, different nations and cultures. The famous architect and inventor R. Buckminster Fuller and the late educator Marshall McLuhan have stressed that electronic communications is turning the world into a global village.

Ready or not, you've been catapulted into a new framework dominated by communications. You live in volatile times, straddling catastrophe and the millenia. How well you do personally is related to the quality of your vocabulary.

Use a word carelessly and the chances are that the thought behind the word was careless too. Thought and language are like fraternal twins; not identical, but very closely related. Words form the core of thought, and so the limitations of your vocabulary will mark the limitations of your thought.

When you think about it, we treat words in a strange way. They're among the most precious possessions of our civilized life. In fact without them there would be no civilization. They came first: "In the beginning was the Word." Yet, most of the time we treat them as casually and carelessly as the air we pollute.

The more you master words, the more control you have over your life. You're not as apt to be bamboozled by the ridiculous jargon too often found in academic and bureaucratic writing and speaking. You're in a healthier position to understand and evaluate what you read and hear. You'll be more comfortable in meetings and find it easier to speak, for you'll have a good grasp of what's happening and the words you need to make yourself clear.

A well-founded vocabulary is similar to having a sizable bank account. It's your passbook to a better self-expression of your personality. It's your protection against mental poverty, freeing you from the shackles that poverty of any kind imposes. The proof has been in for years that people with stronger vocabularies almost always have a more successful life.

This is why SUPER WORD POWER will be a helpful guide, for it combines entertaining and informative articles that will give you new insights into language with the internationally popular quiz "It Pays To Enrich Your Word Power," all selected from issues of *Reader's Digest*.

How Big is Your Vocabulary?

There are various estimates as to the possible number of

words individuals know or at least recognize. So much depends on your education, your interests and your reading habits. People who read more generally have a larger mental dictionary.

When I encourage you to increase your word power by building an up-to-date vocabulary, I have in mind a somewhat selective one. After all, you do have over a million words to choose from, and the average adult recognizes about 50,000 to 60,000 of them.

How do you go about selecting? First of all remember that about 400,000 words are scientific or technical. Some of them you will know because they may be related to your profession or specific interests. Many of the remaining 600,000 are made up of different parts of speech of the same word, such as *trauma, traumatic, traumatically, traumatize, etc.* Then there are rare and exotic words you'd seldom use, as well as the names of people, cities and the like. Take one more step and cut out the simple words, the *ands, buts, ifs, etc.*

By this time you'll be tapping a reservoir of perhaps 150,000 words. How many of them will you add to your mental dictionary? Ideally, the more the better. Your brain is an interconnected network of information and every addition becomes related to the whole in a miraculous way. Learning a word is not adding just one more unit of information. Rather, a synergistic effect evolves, where that unit in its connection with related units creates an entirely new quantity and quality of information.

Realistically, however, you have to continue your selectivity to build a vocabulary that's current and broadly useful. I've estimated that the heart of our English language—apart from the simple and technical words—resides in about 12,000 words. This is where you will find SUPER WORD POWER of practical use. You will be encountering 660 of these words. Many may be new and you will add them to your store. With others, like old friends you've known in the past, you will be reestablishing an acquaintance.

The good news from psychologists is that apparently your ability to learn can remain steady, perhaps even increase, throughout your life. And what is one of the surest and most enjoyable ways to expand your brain power? By continuing to enrich your word power. These articles and quizzes should aid you in this endeavor.

Two Words to Avoid, Two to Remember

By ARTHUR GORDON

Nothing in life is more exciting and rewarding than the sudden flash of insight that leaves you a changed person—not only changed, but changed for the better. Such moments are rare, certainly, but they come to all of us. Sometimes from a book, a sermon, a line of poetry. Sometimes from a friend. . . .

That wintry afternoon in Manhattan, waiting in the little French restaurant, I was feeling frustrated and depressed. Because of several miscalculations on my part, a project of considerable importance in my life had fallen through. Even the prospect of seeing a dear friend (the Old Man, as I privately and affectionately thought of him) failed to cheer me as it usually did. I sat there frowning at the checkered tablecloth, chewing the bitter cud of hindsight.

He came across the street, finally, muffled in his ancient overcoat, shapeless felt hat pulled down over his bald head, looking more like an energetic gnome than an eminent psychiatrist. His offices were nearby; I knew he had just left his last patient of the day. He was close to 80, but he still carried a full case load, still acted as director of a large foundation, still loved to escape to the golf course whenever he could.

By the time he came over and sat beside me, the waiter had brought his invariable bottle of ale. I had not seen him for several months, but he seemed as indestructible as ever. "Well, young man," he said without preliminary, "what's troubling you?"

I had long since ceased to be surprised at his perceptiveness. So I proceeded to tell him, at some length, just what was bothering me. With a kind of melancholy pride, I tried to be very honest. I blamed no one else for my disappointment, only myself. I analyzed the whole thing, all the bad judgments, the false moves. I went on for perhaps 15 minutes, while the Old Man sipped his ale in silence.

When I finished, he put down his glass. "Come on," he said. "Let's go back to my office."

"Your office? Did you forget something?"

"No," he said mildly. "I want your reaction to something. That's all."

A chill rain was beginning to fall outside, but his office was warm and comfortable and familiar: book-lined walls, long leather couch, signed photograph of Sigmund Freud, tape recorder by the window. His secretary had gone home. We were alone.

The Old Man took a tape from a flat cardboard box and fitted it onto the machine. "On this tape," he said, "are three short recordings made by three persons who came to me for help. They are not identified, of course. I want you to listen to the recordings and see if you can pick out the two-word phrase that is the common denominator in all three cases." He smiled. "Don't look so puzzled. I have my reasons."

What the owners of the voices on the tape had in common, it seemed to me, was unhappiness. The man who spoke first evidently had suffered some kind of business loss or failure; he berated himself for not having worked harder, for not having looked ahead. The woman who spoke next had never married because of a sense of obligation to her widowed mother; she recalled bitterly all the marital chances she had let go by. The third voice belonged to a mother whose teen-age son was in trouble with the police; she blamed herself endlessly.

The Old Man switched off the machine and leaned back in

his chair. "Six times in those recordings a phrase is used that's full of a subtle poison. Did you spot it? No? Well, perhaps that's because you used it three times yourself down in the restaurant a little while ago." He picked up the box that had held the tape and tossed it over to me. "There they are, right on the label. The two saddest words in any language."

I looked down. Printed neatly in red ink were the words: *If only.*

"You'd be amazed," said the Old Man, "if you knew how many thousands of times I've sat in this chair and listened to woeful sentences beginning with those two words. 'If only,' they say to me, 'I had done it differently—or not done it at all. If only I hadn't lost my temper, said that cruel thing, made that dishonest move, told that foolish lie. If only I had been wiser, or more unselfish, or more self-controlled.' They go on and on until I stop them. Sometimes I make them listen to the recordings you just heard. 'If only,' I say to them, 'you'd stop saying *if only,* we might begin to get somewhere!'"

The Old Man stretched out his legs. "The trouble with 'if only,'" he said, "is that it doesn't change anything. It keeps the person facing the wrong way—backward instead of forward. It wastes time. In the end, if you let it become a habit, it can become a real roadblock, an excuse for not trying anymore.

"Now take your own case: your plans didn't work out. Why? Because you made certain mistakes. Well, that's all right: everyone makes mistakes. Mistakes are what we learn from. But when you were telling me about them, lamenting this, regretting that, you weren't really learning from them."

"How do you know?" I said, a bit defensively.

"Because," said the Old Man, "you never got out of the past tense. Not once did you mention the future. And in a way— be honest, now!—you were enjoying it. There's a perverse streak in all of us that makes us like to hash over old mistakes. After all, when you relate the story of some disaster or disappointment that has happened to you, you're still the chief character, still in the center of the stage."

I shook my head ruefully. "Well, what's the remedy?"

"Shift the focus," said the Old Man promptly. "Change the key words and substitute a phrase that supplies lift instead of creating drag."

"Do you have such a phrase to recommend?"

"Certainly. Strike out the words 'if only'; substitute the phrase 'next time.'"

"Next time?"

"That's right. I've seen it work minor miracles right here in this room. As long as a patient keeps saying 'if only' to me, he's in trouble. But when he looks me in the eye and says 'next time,' I know he's on his way to overcoming his problem. It means he has decided to apply the lessons he has learned from his experience, however grim or painful it may have been. It means he's going to push aside the roadblock of regret, move forward, take action, resume living. Try it yourself. You'll see."

My old friend stopped speaking. Outside, I could hear the rain whispering against the windowpane. I tried sliding one phrase out of my mind and replacing it with the other. It was fanciful, of course, but I could hear the new words lock into place with an audible click.

"One last thing," the Old Man said. "Apply this little trick to things that can still be remedied." From the bookcase behind him he pulled out something that looked like a diary. "Here's a journal kept a generation ago by a woman who was a schoolteacher in my hometown. Her husband was a kind of amiable ne'er-do-well, charming but totally inadequate as a provider. This woman had to raise the children, pay the bills, keep the family together. Her diary is full of angry references to Jonathan's weaknesses, Jonathan's shortcomings, Jonathan's inadequacies.

"Then Jonathan died, and all the entries ceased except for one—years later. Here it is: 'Today I was made superintendent of schools, and I suppose I should be very proud. But if I knew that Jonathan was out there somewhere beyond the stars, and if I knew how to manage it, I would go to him tonight.'"

The Old Man closed the book gently. "You see? What she's saying is 'if only'; if only I had accepted him, faults and all; if only I had loved him while I could." He put the book back on the shelf. "That's when those sad words are the saddest of all: when it's too late to retrieve anything."

He stood up a bit stiffly. "Well, class dismissed. It has been good to see you, young man. Always is. Now, if you will help me find a taxi, I probably should be getting on home."

We came out of the building into the rainy night. I spotted a cruising cab and ran toward it, but another pedestrian was quicker.

"My, my," said the Old Man slyly. "If only we had come down ten seconds sooner, we'd have caught that cab, wouldn't we?"

I laughed and picked up the cue. "Next time I'll run faster."

"That's it," cried the Old Man, pulling his absurd hat down around his ears. "That's it exactly!"

Another taxi slowed. I opened the door for him. He smiled and waved as it moved away. I never saw him again. A month later, he died of a sudden heart attack, in full stride, so to speak.

Several years have passed since that rainy afternoon in Manhattan. But to this day, whenever I find myself thinking "if only," I change it to "next time." Then I wait for that almost-perceptible mental click. And when I hear it, I think of the Old Man.

A small fragment of immortality, to be sure. But it's the kind he would have wanted.

Word Power Test No. 1

Winston Churchill

By PETER FUNK

Sir Winston Churchill was known as a master of the English language who roused, cajoled, admonished and conciliated people of all nations during an era of unparalleled tribulation. He used strong words to convey his vigorous thoughts. These test words are taken from his speeches during World War II. Choose the word or phrase nearest in meaning to the key word. Check your results at the end of this test.

1. **imponderable** (im pon′ der uh b'l)—A: manifest. B: confining. C: incapable of being evaluated. D: meditative.
2. **retaliate** (re tăl′ ē āt)—A: to repeat. B: add on. C: repay in kind. D: nullify.
3. **cede** (sēd)—A: to impregnate. B: begin. C: retreat. D: yield.
4. **vitiate** (vish′ ē āt)—A: to impair. B: reject. C: quicken. D: enhance.
5. **acumen** (a kū′ men)—A: accuracy. B: shrewdness. C: force. D: obtuseness.

6. **temerity** (te mair′ i tē)—A: fear. B: recklessness. C: diffidence. D: ruthlessness.

7. **fabricate** (fab′ rĭ cāt)—A: to stretch. B: concoct. C: indulge. D: dazzle.

8. **juncture** (junk′ chur)—A: beginning. B: obstruction. C: critical moment. D: complexity.

9. **calumny** (kăl′ um nē)—A: cleverness. B: hardship. C: compliment. D: slander.

10. **verbiage** (ver′ bē ĭj)—A: fecundity. B: precision. C: wordiness. D: foliage.

11. **blandishment** (blan′ dish ment)—A: nonsense. B: threat. C: abrasion. D: flattery.

12. **ignoble** (ig nō′ b′l)—A: aloof. B: unknown. C: bizarre. D: dishonorable.

13. **compass** (kum′ pass)—A: passageway. B: point. C: scope. D: restriction.

14. **daunt**—A: to intimidate. B: overwhelm. C: dare. D: show off.

15. **brazen** (brā′ z′n)—A: glowing. B: unbreakable. C: irresponsible. D: shameless.

16. **legion** (lē′ jun)—A: distance. B: rampage. C: multitude. D: motto.

17. **arrears** (uh rĭrz′)—A: disorientation. B: throwback. C: holding pattern. D: unfulfilled obligations.

18. **deployment** (de ploy′ ment)—A: dismissal. B: spreading out. C: seizure. D: judgment.

19. **subvention** (sub ven′ shun)—A: deception. B: subsidy. C: evasion. D: descent.

20. **resilient** (rē zĭl′ yent)—A: rebounding. B: animated. C: resourceful. D: tenacious.

ANSWERS

1. **imponderable**—C: Incapable of being evaluated or measured precisely; as, "the *imponderable* results of our decisions." Latin *imponderabilis* (not weighable).

2. **retaliate**—C: To repay in kind; as, "to *retaliate* with new import quotas." Latin *retaliare*.

3. **cede**—D: To yield or surrender; give up. "You have *ceded* the ports to them." Latin *cedere*.

4. **vitiate**—A: To impair the quality, character or effectiveness of; invalidate. "To violate neutrality may *vitiate* the Allied cause." Latin *vitiare*.

5. **acumen**—B: Shrewdness; keen perception; as, "his legal *acumen*." Latin (the sharp point of anything).

6. **temerity**—B: Recklessness; rash contempt for danger; fool-hardiness. Latin *termeritas*. "We must not underrate the *temerity* of the enemy."

7. **fabricate**—B: To concoct; make up a false account; as, "the *fabricated* story of a plot." Latin *fabricari* (to form, forge).

8. **juncture**—C: Critical moment; turning point. Latin *junctura* (a joining). "There was danger of war at this *juncture*."

9. **calumny**—D: Slander; false and malicious statement intended to damage a reputation; as, "the propaganda of *calumny* and lies." Latin *calumnia* (trickery).

10. **verbiage**—C: Wordiness; as, "to strip the speech of its *verbiage*." Old French *verbier* (to chatter).

11. **blandishment**—D: Flattery; remark or action intended to persuade or coax. Latin *blandiri* (to flatter). "Such *blandishments* have been the prelude to violence."

12. **ignoble**—D: Dishonorable; unworthy. "It is not from any *ignoble* shrinking from pain we pray for peace." Latin *ignobilis*.

13. **compass**—C: Scope; extent or reach; as, "not beyond the *compass* and strength of Great Britain." Old French *compasser* (to go around).

14. **daunt**—A: To intimidate; cause to lose courage when it is needed; as, "[enemy] numbers do not *daunt* us." Latin *domitare* (to tame).

15. **brazen**—D: Shameless; unscrupulous; as, "behind the *brazen* front of the enemy." Old English *braes* (brass).

16. **legion**—C: Originally a Roman military force of 6000 soldiers; therefore, any large number; a multitude; as, "Those who have faith in our sailormen are *legion*." Latin *legere* (to collect).

17. **arrears**—D: Unfulfilled obligations; overdue debts. Latin *ad* (to) and *retro* (behind). "The air programs were falling into *arrears*."

18. **deployment**—B: Spreading out, as of troops, into a more open formation; strategic arrangement; as, "the *deployment* of enemy ships." Latin *displicare* (to unfold).

19. **subvention**—B: Subsidy or grant of money to provide as-
     sistance; as, "a state *subvention*." Latin *subvenire* (to come
     to help).
20. **resilient**—A: Rebounding; springing back into shape; able
     to recover from trouble; as, "the *resilient* strength of Brit-
     ain." Latin *resilire*.

VOCABULARY RATINGS

20—18 correct ....master (exceptional)
17—13 correct .... player (excellent)
12—9 correct ....novice (good)

The Secret Life of James Thurber

By JAMES THURBER

Two years ago, looking for a house to buy, I called at a real estate office. A member of the firm, scrabbling through a box containing keys, looked up to say, "The key to the Roxbury house isn't here, but a skeleton will let you in."

I was suddenly once again five years old, with wide eyes and open mouth. I pictured the Roxbury house as I would have pictured it as a small boy, a house full of dark and nameless horrors.

It was of sentences like that, nonchalantly tossed off by real estate dealers, great-aunts, clergymen and others that the enchanted private world of my early boyhood was made. In this world, businessmen who phoned their wives around five o'clock in the afternoon to say that they were tied up at the office sat roped to their swivel chairs, unable to move. Then there was the man who left town under a cloud. Usually I saw the cloud, about the size of a sofa, floating three or four feet above his head and following him wherever he went.

I remember the grotesque creature who haunted my meditations when my mother said to my father, "Mrs. Johnson was all ears." There were many other wonderful figures in the secret landscapes of my youth: the old lady who was always up in the air, the husband who did not seem able to put his foot down, the man who lost his head during a fire but was still able to run out of the house yelling, the young lady who was, in reality, a soiled dove. One had to brood over this world in silence; if you put it to the test of questions, your parents would try to laugh the miracles away.

Such a world, alas, is not yearproof. It began to dissolve one day when our cook said, "Frances is up in the front room crying her heart out." The fact that a person could cry so hard that his heart would come out of his body, as perfectly shaped and glossy as a red velvet pincushion, was news to me. I went upstairs and opened the door of the front room. Frances jumped off the bed and ran downstairs.

I tore the bed apart and kicked up the rugs, searching for her heart. It was no good. I looked out the window at the rain and the darkening sky. My cherished mental image of the man under the cloud began to grow dim and fade away. Downstairs, in the living room, Frances was still crying. I began to laugh.

Word Power Test No. 2

Our Picturesque Language

By PETER FUNK

In ancient Egypt, the hieroglyph 𓀁 meant "to rejoice." And 𓃗
—a giraffe peering into the distance—meant "to foretell." Today,
nearly 5000 years later, many of our words still have pictures
hidden inside. In fact, each of the words in the test below embodies
a picture, although not so obviously as the ancient hieroglyphs.
Check the word or phrase you believe is nearest in meaning to the
key words. Answers appear after this test.

1. **broach** (brōch)—A: to decorate. B: bridge. C: offend. D:
   introduce.
2. **cynosure** (sī′ nō sure)—A: obscurity. B: center of attention.
   C: certainty. D: clown.
3. **vicissitude** (vĭ sis′ ĭ tūd)—A: danger. B: change of fortune.
   C: complexity. D: evil.
4. **hazardous** (hăz′ ar dus)—A: unintentional. B: unprotected.
   C: risky. D: doubtful.
5. **pithy** (pith′ ē)—A: witty. B: tenacious. C: ribald. D: succinct.

6. **scavenger** (skav′ in jer)—A: minor noble. B: junkman. C: burglar. D: counselor.

7. **fetid** (fĕt′ id)—A: doomed. B: dangerous. C: stinking. D: disease-breeding.

8. **pugnacious** (pug nā′ shus)—A: homely. B: stubborn. C: persistent. D: truculent.

9. **rankle** (rang′ k'l)—A: argue noisily. B: warp. C: cause continued resentment. D: confuse.

10. **feline** (fē′ līne)—A: clumsy. B: curving. C: loyal. D: cat-like.

11. **cynicism** (sin′ ĭs iz'm)—A: grumpiness. B: sneering disbelief. C: benevolence. D: cleverness.

12. **ambush** (am′ bush)—A: to drive out. B: denounce. C: make a surprise attack. D: cut away undergrowth.

13. **oscillate** (os′ ĭ late)—A: to kiss. B: swing back and forth. C: electrify. D: dissemble.

14. **crucial** (krōō′ shul)—A: exceptional. B: tragic. C: critical and decisive. D: insistent.

15. **stodgy** (stōj′ ē)—A: sturdy. B: dull. C: blunt. D: obstinate.

16. **catapult** (kat′ ă pult)—A: to hurl. B: climb. C: crawl. D: fall.

17. **tirade** (tī′ rāde)—A: conciliation. B: afterthought. C: forceful action. D: angry speech.

18. **turgid** (tur′ jid)—A: bloated. B: muddy. C: unruly. D: concealed.

19. **aloof** (a lōōf′)—A: sociable. B: high. C: detached. D: conservative.

20. **fledgling** (flej′ ling)—A person who is A: placid. B: overconfident. C: enthusiastic. D: young and inexperienced.

ANSWERS

1. **broach**—D: Introduce; mention or suggest for the first time. To *broach* a topic of conversation is to "pierce" it open or "bite" into it. Middle English *broche* (spike, spear), from Latin *broccus* (projection of teeth).

2. **cynosure**—B: Center of attention or admiration. Latin *Cynosura* (Ursa Minor constellation containing the Pole Star, which every ancient navigator looked to for guidance).

3. **vicissitude**—B: Change of fortune; fluctuation in condition,

as of wealth or poverty, success or failure; as, the vicissitudes of life. Latin *vicis* (change).

4. **hazardous**—C: Subject to high risk or danger; as, a *hazardous* mission. From Arabic *al-zahr* (dice game), via Spanish *azar* (unforeseen disaster) into Middle French *hasard*.

5. **pithy**—D: Succinct; concise; having substance and point; tersely cogent; as, a *pithy* proverb. Old English *pitha* (pith, marrow).

6. **scavenger**—B: Junkman; person who culls through refuse. Also, any animal eating decayed matter. From Middle English *scavage* (a toll), to *scavager* (tax collector), to *scavenger* (supervisor of street cleaning).

7. **fetid**—C: Stinking; having a foul odor as of rot or decay; as, a *fetid* pond. Latin *foetere* (to stink).

8. **pugnacious**—D: A *pugnacious* person is truculent, belligerent, ready to fight. Latin *pugnus* (fist).

9. **rankle**—C: An insult *rankles:* it causes a bitterness like that of a festering sore or the biting of little teeth. Medieval Latin *dracunculus* (ulcer), from Greek *drakon* (serpent).

10. **feline**—D: Cat-like; sly; stealthy; as, *feline* grace. Latin *felinus* (cat).

11. **cynicism**—B: Sneering disbelief; skepticism. Certain Greek philosophers who taught simplicity and virtue became so self-righteous that they were called *hoi kynikoi* (the snarlers), from *kynikos* (dog-like).

12. **ambush**—C: To make a surprise attack from a concealed position. Old French *embuschier* (take to the woods).

13. **oscillate**—B: To swing back and forth like a pendulum; to vibrate. Latin *oscillum* (a small mask of Bacchus hanging as a vineyard scarecrow, swinging in the wind).

14. **crucial**—C: Critical and decisive; relating to a supreme trial or final choice. Latin *crux* (cross, in the sense of a "crossroad").

15. **stodgy**—B: Dull; stuffy; uninteresting. A *stodgy* person resembles the English *stodge* (a heavy, thick and sometimes indigestible pudding).

16. **catapult**—A: To hurl forward. Latin *catapulta* (ancient military device for throwing arrows and rocks).

17. **tirade**—D: Long, angry, denunciatory speech. Literally a "volley" of words. Italian *tirata* (discharge of firearms).

18. **turgid**—A: Bloated; swollen; inflated; as, a *turgid* literary style. Latin *turgere* (to swell).

19. **aloof**—C: Detached, cool or distant in manner. From a Dutch nautical term *aloufe* (to steer clear of the shore).

20. **fledgling**—D: A young, inexperienced person, like the young bird that has just got its flying feathers. Middle English *flegge* (feathered).

VOCABULARY RATINGS

20—18 correct .... master (exceptional)

17—13 correct .... player (excellent)

12—9 correct .... novice (good)

How to Say It in Writing

Listen to an office telephone conversation, and you may hear something like this: "Hello, Mr. James. This is Joe Connolly at Ace. Say, we're sorry about that order. The factory shipped to the wrong warehouse, but you'll have the stuff Friday."

Now let us assume that Connolly decides to write rather than call James. The letter may well come out this way:

Dear Mr. James:

Your letter of April 15 requesting information on your order has been received.

Our shipments to your warehouse are in the normal course made directly from the factory, as you know. In this instance, however, due to an improper routing of the invoices, the delivery was made to our warehouse. We have searched the warehouse and found your entire shipment.

This is to inform you that we will deliver it this Friday. We regret any inconvenience this delay may have caused you.

In going from speaking to writing, Joe Connolly appears to have been transformed. On the phone he was brief and to the point; in the letter he became stuffy and long-winded, as many people do when they are called upon to write a letter, do an article for a club bulletin or draw up a memorandum for the boss. Suddenly they start using high-flown words and twisted sentences. And the results either bore or confuse their readers.

Many companies have brought in experts to teach employes how to write understandable English. Federal agencies and the Army and Air Force also conduct writing programs. The problem of clear, simple communication is so widespread you might conclude that only a specially gifted person can write clearly. This is not so.

All you have to do is apply basic rules of good writing. Here are several important ones.

Remember Your Reader. What does the person who is going to read your material already know of your subject? An economist writing for colleagues could get away with, "Extrapolation of current data indicates that market forces should attain equilibrium at an annual sales rate of two million units." For laymen, however, he might better say, "Sales should stabilize at two million units a year."

It is equally important to determine what your audience *wants* to know. If your employer, for example, sends you somewhere to investigate a proposed factory site, would you, in your report, tell him that you traveled by plane, stayed the first night at a motel, the second at a hotel, hired a car to drive around, etc.? Not if you value your reputation. The boss wants your recommendations, not a travelogue. True, he has to look at the memo. But if it begins this way, he may later skip over vital points. Many letters remain forever half-read, many reports half-understood, because the writer was more interested in himself than in the reader.

Decide What to Say. The unskilled writer frequently thinks sentence by sentence. By the time he arrives at Sentence 10, he discovers that it should have followed Sentence 3. The remedy: list your major points beforehand in the sequence that will make the most sense. For a short letter or memo, jot down only the central thoughts. For more extensive writing, make an outline.

Suppose your PTA asked you to evaluate the need for additional space at your children's school. Your report could be put into this outline:

1. Present capacity of school: 1500
2. Current enrollment: 1496
3. Estimated enrollment 1964: 1712. 1982: 1973
4. Present plans for new students
    a. Board of Education had $2,300,000 allocated in last budget for school addition.
    b. Request was turned down by County Council.
    c. Board of Education has included same appropriation in new budget.
5. Possible action
    a. At next County Council hearings on education budget we could request approval of appropriation.
    b. Put issue before next PTA meeting.

Be Brief and Simple. Amateur writers too often equate length with significance; the longer the letter or article, the weightier it seems.

"The scope of the broad objective of this survey was primarily to investigate and assess the potential in Iraq for the development of a chemical industry in the private sector." What is the writer laboring to say in those 30 words? "The survey's primary objective was to assess the potential for a private chemical industry in Iraq." Isn't that—in 16 words—the essential thought? The author would never have wandered so far from his point if he had observed these precautions:

Say It Once, Not Twice. Don't repeat yourself unless it's required for emphasis. In the chemical-survey example, isn't it reasonable to assume that the subject would be investigated before it was assessed?

Avoid Roundabout Expressions. You can tighten a sentence by eliminating surplus words and sometimes by changing the verb from passive form to active. Instead of, "This is to notify you that your letter was received," why not, "We received your letter"? An active verb, furthermore, usually carries more punch.

Stick to Familiar Words. This does not mean you must renounce words of more than three syllables. However, don't use big words unless they sharpen your thought. In the previous sentence, for example, would "utilize" in place of "use" have helped your understanding?

Keep Sentences Short. When you find a sentence running away, stop it with a period or semicolon. Don't let paragraphs run too long: a large block of print tires the reader.

We always marvel at the ease with which a skilled person in any field exercises his craft. Yet even the man with superb talent has to develop it through hard work. Writing is no different from other skills; you can't expect well-formed prose just to drop from your pen. Go over everything you write at least once and test it against the rules. Try saying the same thing with fewer and simpler words. The odds are that you will find your writing coming to life.

Word Power Test No. 3

A Sporting Chance

By PETER FUNK

When your favorite reporters or newscasters describe this fall's sports events, they might well use words like these, selected from the pages of *Reader's Digest*. Pick the answer you think is correct, then check your results at the end of this test.

1. **rowdy**—A: rough and disorderly. B: kind. C: sedate. D: late.
2. **persevere** (pur su VIR)—A: to equalize. B: persist. C: quit. D: urge.
3. **procure** (prō CURE)—A: to heal. B: induce. C: obtain. D: hold back.
4. **sear**—A: to cast a horoscope. B: languish. C: flare up. D: cause to wither or scorch.
5. **botch**—A: to bungle. B: hit. C: refine. D: prevent.
6. **grapple** (GRAP ul)—A: to push. B: impress. C: provoke. D: grasp.
7. **straddle** (STRAD 'l)—A: to bring to a halt. B: have one leg on either side of. C: tie up. D: travel aimlessly.

23

8. **seethe**—A: to sigh. B: remain inert. C: be extremely upset. D: run.

9. **bicker**—A: to bargain. B: offend. C: fret. D: squabble.

10. **quicksilver**—A: unpredictable or mercurial. B: sleazy. C: honorable. D: of questionable integrity.

11. **bona fide** (BŌ nuh fīde)—A: secured by a bond. B: comfortably situated. C: in good faith. D: bogus.

12. **scrabble**—A: to be mean. B: mix in a confused way. C: become cool. D: scrape or scratch at hurriedly.

13. **counter**—A: to consider carefully. B: link together. C: oppose. D: place on top of one another.

14. **hover** (HUV ur; HOV ur)—A: to remain in the air above one spot. B: shake or move gently. C: cover carefully. D: submerge.

15. **disoriented** (dis OR ē ent id)—A: freed from illusion. B: organized. C: excluded from a group. D: having lost a sense of direction.

16. **swath**—A: a long, open strip. B: widespread destruction. C: sample piece of cloth. D: type of headdress.

17. **attribute** (uh TRIB yōōt)—A: to praise or admire. B: study. C: give proof of. D: assign or ascribe to.

18. **execrable** (EK suh kruh b'l)—A: hard. B: detestable. C: painful. D: fine.

19. **nostrum** (NOS trum)—A: theory. B: quack medicine. C: raised platform. D: animus.

20. **slue**—A: to lag behind. B: twist or skid. C: pronounce indistinctly. D: drain off.

ANSWERS

1. **rowdy**—A: Rough and disorderly; as, *rowdy* spectators. Perhaps related to *row* (noisy dispute).

2. **persevere**—B: To persist or continue in spite of difficulties or obstacles; as, the will to *persevere* to the end. Latin *perseverare*.

3. **procure**—C: To obtain or acquire by effort; as, They *procured* films of the disputed play. Latin *procurare* (to take care of).

4. **sear**—D: To cause to scorch or dry up; as, The burning sun daily *seared* the playing fields. Old English *searian* (to become withered).

5. **botch**—A: To bungle; spoil by clumsiness, careless work or ineptitude; as, to *botch* an extra point kick. Uncertain origin.

6. **grapple**—D: To grasp or take hold of firmly; figuratively, to struggle with mentally; as, to *grapple* with a difficult problem. Provençal *grapa* (hook).

7. **straddle**—B: To sit or stand with one leg on either side of; figuratively, to seem to favor both sides of an issue.

8. **seethe**—C: From Old English *seothan* (to boil); hence, to be extremely upset or agitated.

9. **bicker**—D: To squabble; quarrel about unimportant matters; as, They *bickered* about where they'd sit on the bench. Middle English *bikeren* (to skirmish).

10. **quicksilver**—A: Unpredictable and mercurial; as, a *quicksilver* temper. Another name for liquid mercury from the way it moves and looks.

11. **bona fide**—C: Done in good faith; with sincerity; as, a *bona fide* offer. Also authentic or genuine. Literal translation from Latin.

12. **scrabble**—D: To scrape, scratch at or grope for, often hurriedly or frantically; as, The climber's fingers *scrabbled* against the cliff for a place to hold. Middle Dutch *schrabben* (to scrape).

13. **counter**—C: To oppose; make an opposite move; as, The striking players *countered* with an added demand. Latin *contra* (against).

14. **hover**—A: A *hovering* bird remains in the air above one place. Middle English *hoveren* (to linger).

15. **disoriented**—D: Having lost a sense of direction; confused about time, place or identity; literally, turning away from the east. Latin *dis-* (away) and *oriens* (east).

16. **swath**—A: A long, open strip; as, a *swath* of grass cut by a mower. Old English *swaeth* (width of a scythe's cutting sweep).

17. **attribute**—D: To assign or ascribe to; as, *attributing* an error to the shortstop. Latin *attribuere*.

18. **execrable**—B: Detestable; horrifying; as, an *execrable* crime. Also of very poor quality. Latin *exsecrari* (to curse).

19. **nostrum**—B: Quack medicine; favorite remedy; cure-all; as, a *nostrum* for a tennis elbow. Latin *nostrum* (of our own make).

20. **slue**—B: To twist; swing about; veer; skid out of a course

or direction; as, The racing car *slued* to the right. Origin unknown.

VOCABULARY RATINGS

20—18 correct ....master (exceptional)

17—13 correct .... player (excellent)

12—9 correct ....novice (good)

Unforgettable Perry Mason

The question of where former trial lawyer Erle Stanley Gardner left off and his detective-story hero began is practically unanswerable

By JAMES STEWART-GORDON

To chief deputy prosecutor Darrell R. Parker of Maricopa County, Ariz., the 1941 murder case against Frank Pass should have been perfect: he had the weapon, a bloodstained hammer, and a willing witness. But the witness was the wife of the accused killer, and Arizona law said Mrs. Pass could not testify against her husband without his consent.

Worn-out with rerunning the case through his mind, Parker turned for relaxation to a detective novel, *The Case of the Curious Bride,* by Erle Stanley Gardner. As Parker read, he found that hero Perry Mason, a lawyer-cum-detective, was faced with a problem opposite to that which bedeviled Parker—how to prevent the court from accepting the testimony of a husband against a wife. The prosecutor in Mason's case tried to annul the marriage, thus opening the way for her husband to testify. Mason showed the marriage to be legal, thereby blocking the husband's testimony. Parker felt a sense of excitement. *What if Pass and his wife were not legally married?*

Parker checked the accused's marriage records and discovered Pass had enough Indian blood to classify him as a Paiute. His wife, though part-Mexican, was legally a Caucasian, and an Arizona statute made such a marriage illegal. Subsequently, the testimony of Mrs. Pass was admitted in court, and the killer was convicted. Perry Mason, reaching out from a book into real life, had scored again.

Since his first appearance in March 1933 in *The Case of the Velvet Claws,* Perry Mason has become the most successful fictional sleuth of modern times. He never lost a case, and the sales of his 82 action-packed adventures have compiled records which may never be surpassed. To date, more than 310 million Erle Stanley Gardner thrillers have been sold, with Mason's exploits having been translated into 37 languages. Although no new Perry Mason adventure has appeared since 1973, every 24 hours 2000 Mason books are purchased.

Dramatizations of the Mason stories, with Raymond Burr playing the title role, ran for nine years on U.S. television, have been seen in more than 62 foreign countries and are still widely shown in Brazil, Latin America and the United States. On radio, Mason appeared five times a week for 12 years and now is being considered for a new series. Mason was the hero of half a dozen movies until Gardner withdrew permission because he felt Hollywood didn't understand his hero.

Perry's fans do. They know his weapons are: the greatest courtroom presence since Daniel Webster, an encyclopedic knowledge of California law, and the undivided loyalty of private detective Paul Drake and secretary Della Street. Most frequently his courtroom opponent is Hamilton "Ham" Burger, the imaginary district attorney of Los Angeles County. Time after time, Burger and his fellow prosecutors believe that they have an airtight case; but Mason, with his mastery of legal witchcraft and deadly skill as a cross-examiner, finds a way to unmask the real villain in the courtroom.

Even when the district attorney thinks he has an unimpeachable eye-witness, Mason has a counterstroke. In *The Case of the Howling Dog,* Bessie Forbes, Mason's innocent client, is accused of murder because she has taken a taxi to the scene of the crime and left a handkerchief drenched in perfume on the back seat. Knowing that the prosecution will use the cabdriver to identify Mrs. Forbes, Perry hires an actress who resembles his client, and douses her with "Vol de Nuit" (the scent on the hankie). He then sends the actress to get the handkerchief from the cabdriver. In court, Mason destroys the cabbie's testimony by making him admit that if he is mistaken as to the identity of the woman who retrieved the handkerchief, he may be also wrong about the identity of his original fare. When the driver maintains that it was Bessie Forbes who picked up the hankie, Mason is on his way to proving his client's innocence. None of Mason's clients are ever guilty, of course. Most of them are beautiful women on the warm side of 30 with splendid legs and kissable mouths, who by some mischance have fallen afoul of California law.

Almost every one of Mason's adventures is based on a legal principle or was suggested by a case which Erle Stanley Gardner, a California trial lawyer himself, used in court. The question of where the creator leaves off and where the creation begins is practically unanswerable.

Gardner was born July 17, 1889, in Malden, Mass., but by the time he was 13 the Gardners had moved to California, where Erle spent the rest of his life. He combined high school with work as a typist in a Palo Alto law firm and later studied law on his own. In 1911, at the age of 21, he was admitted to the bar, and the prototype adventures of Perry Mason in the person of Erle Stanley Gardner began.

In 1913, Gardner started practicing in Oxnard, a small California town with a sizable Chinese population. Stocky, bespectacled Erle, a born defender of the underdog and student of the most obscure dodges in the state's criminal code, became their champion.

On one occasion, he was hired to defend 20 Chinese about to be charged with selling lottery tickets. Knowing the out-of-town detective hired to arrest the Chinese was unable to tell one Oriental from another, Gardner moved each of the accused from his accustomed place of business to a new locale. Wong Duck, the butcher, was put in Ah Lee's laundry, and the other 18 were also shifted. At the police station, the detective incorrectly identified all of them. At the trial, Gardner pointed out that if the arresting officer was not able to tell one Chinese from another, how could he know who had been selling lottery tickets? The case was dismissed and Gardner became a Chinatown hero.

The repercussions of the case were manifold. Gardner eventually learned enough Cantonese to chat confidently with his new clients, earned the name Da Zhuang Shi (great lawyer) and developed material for his story plots. Some years later, he made a trip to China, where he was treated by his hosts like visiting royalty. But during his travels he was also placed under house arrest, accused of being a spy, and pursued by pirates, who had never heard of the great Da Zhuang Shi from California.

In 1921, on impulse, Gardner decided to try writing fiction to increase his income. Daily he sweated through his legal business. Nights, Gardner, who was later to turn out more than two million words in one year and enter the *Guinness Book of World Records* as the fastest novelist in the world, turned out stories for pulp magazines. Although deluged by rejection slips, at the end of the first two years Gardner, writing under the pseudonym of Charles M. Green, managed to sell a good number of his stories.

Each year both his law practice and his writing success marched forward. In 1926, Gardner, the moonlighting author, sold 35 stories and novelettes, and Gardner, the mouthpiece, continued to pull hopeless cases out of the fire.

Once he defended a $250,000 damage suit brought by a young woman, who claimed her nerves had been shattered by the actions of Gardner's client. This had prevented her marriage and left her a timorous wreck. The client's case looked hopeless until an earthquake struck. As the courtroom rocked, everyone dove under tables and benches—except the claimant and Gardner.

When court resumed, Gardner, in a move worthy of Perry Mason, pointed to the claimant and addressed the jury: "All of you," he said, "were scared. This girl was as cool as a cucumber. Does this look like the action of a woman made timid by anything my client said or did?" Fifteen minutes later the jury came back with a verdict in favor of Gardner's client.

By 1932, Gardner had climbed to the top of the list of penny-a-word Shakespeares who filled the pages of the detective magazines. Even at pulp magazines' modest pay, during the Depression he was earning over $20,000 a year from writing.

It was the advent of the dictating machine that made Perry Mason possible. By dictating, and employing three secretaries,

Gardner was able to turn out an even more massive amount of work. In 1933, when the first two Mason novels appeared, Gardner also published 69 additional novelettes, short stories and magazine articles.

The first Perry Mason book, *The Case of the Velvet Claws*, was dictated by Gardner in 3½ days with part of each day devoted to his legal practice. Rejected by several publishers, it was accepted by William Morrow and Company, and was to prove to be for both Gardner and Morrow the key to the mint. The book has in the past 47 years appeared in 19 U.S. editions and been reprinted in 34 foreign versions, selling over four million copies. New Perry Mason books followed in spaces of two and three a year. A passionate outdoorsman, Uncle Erle, as he liked to be called, equipped a small van with the necessities of survival in the wilds and took to slipping away into the desert with his dictating apparatus, to emerge days later with a new Perry Mason under his belt.

But by 1938 Gardner was beginning to wonder if interest in Perry Mason would one day slacken. Could he duplicate his success by writing a novel with another set of characters? The book, written under the pseudonym of A. A. Fair, was *The Bigger They Come,* and it featured Bertha Cool, an overweight, diamond-ringed, private-detective-agency owner, and her employee, pint-size Donald Lam, a bundle of legal dynamite. The pair scored an immediate success, and Gardner went on to write 29 Cool and Lam books.

In 1947, Gardner was enjoying life and probably the largest income of any writer of his time. Then he received a visit from a young lawyer named Al Matthews. Matthews had a penniless, friendless client, William Marvin Lindley, who had been found guilty of murder. Refused a reprieve by Gov. Earl Warren, Lindley was on his way to the gas chamber. Convinced of his client's innocence, Matthews asked if Gardner could help.

Gardner went to work to save Lindley. Reconstructing the crime, he concluded that the young lawyer was right. Gardner wrote letters setting forth his conclusions to the governor and every justice of the California supreme court. Although Warren, who was out of the state, had ordered that Lindley be given no reprieve, Gardner's letters were so persuasive that the supreme court unanimously requested Lt. Gov. Frederick F. Houser to order a stay of execution. Eventually Governor

Warren, acting on the court's recommendation, commuted the sentence of Lindley, who had since been declared insane, to life imprisonment.

Though Lindley was not technically exonerated, his life was saved and the case convinced Gardner that there were others who needed help and had no place to turn. With the aid of Harry Steeger, publisher of *Argosy* magazine, the Court of Last Resort was formed in 1948—a blue-ribbon panel of experts headed by Gardner, who sifted evidence on questionable cases. During the next ten years, the panel examined hundreds of requests from lawyers and prisoners, managing to save the lives of 33 innocent men and women.

Gardner died in 1970 at age 80, accepted as an international expert on criminal law and showered with honors from his fellow lawyers. He also left behind one of the most crowded and successful lives imaginable. As his final bequest he left the world Perry Mason, who will live forever.

IT PAYS TO ENRICH YOUR WORD POWER ®

Word Power Test No. 4

High School Horrors

By PETER FUNK

In this list of words drawn from high school vocabulary tests, check the word or phrase you believe is *nearest in meaning* to the key word. Answers appear after this test.

1. **paltry** (pawl′ trē)—A: insignificant. B: unfair. C: average. D: slovenly.
2. **disparage** (dis păr′ ij)—A: to scatter. B: discriminate. C: belittle. D: waste.
3. **overture** (ō′ ver tūr)—A: disclosure. B: apology. C: request. D: proposal.
4. **lethargy** (leth′ ar jē)—A: serenity. B: listlessness. C: impassivity. D: laxity.
5. **tractable** (trak′ ta b'l)—A: tillable. B: easily followed. C: understandable. D: docile.
6. **nurture** (nur′ tūr)—A: to ripen. B: pamper. C: nourish. D: relieve.
7. **inchoate** (in kō′ it)—A: loose. B: implicit. C: chaotic. D: incomplete.

8. **satiate** (sā′ shĭ āt)—A: to glut. B: comfort. C: desire. D: water down.

9. **obsession** (ob sesh′ un)—A: dejection. B: preoccupation. C: frustration. D: suspicion.

10. **appease** (a pēz′)—A: to yield. B: give pleasure to. C: placate. D: compromise.

11. **prognosis** (prog nō′ sis)—A: scheme. B: forecast. C: preface. D: identification of a disease.

12. **frenetic** (fre net′ ik)—A: frantic. B: intense. C: passionate. D: fast.

13. **tenable** (ten′ a b'l)—A: experimental. B: long-lasting. C: flimsy. D: defensible.

14. **aperture** (ap′ er tūr)—A: highest point. B: opening. C: pithy phrase. D: arch.

15. **eccentric** (ek sen′ trik)—A: grotesque. B: abnormal. C: unconventional. D: changeable.

16. **precocious** (pre kō′ shus)—A: unusually mature. B: highly prized. C: perceptive. D: scholarly.

17. **graphic** (graf′ ik)—A: moving. B: vivid. C: obvious. D: instructive.

18. **terrestrial** (te res′ trĭ al)—A: widespread. B: relating to the sky. C: windswept. D: earthly.

19. **paroxysm** (par′ ok siz′m)—A: spasm. B: furor. C: paralysis. D: fear.

20. **erosion** (e rō′ zhun)—A: aggravation. B: shallowness. C: deterioration. D: abrasion.

ANSWERS

1. **paltry**—A: Insignificant; trifling; having little or no worth; as, a *paltry* gift. Dialectal English *palt*, (coarse cloth, trash).

2. **disparage**—C: To belittle; speak slightingly of; depreciate; as, to *disparage* another's accomplishments. Old French *desparagier*, (to marry below one's class).

3. **overture**—D: Proposal; first move toward agreement or action; as, a peace *overture*. Middle French *overture*, (opening).

4. **lethargy**—B: Listlessness; abnormal drowsiness; apathy or tired indifference; as, the *lethargy* that comes from poor nutrition. Greek *lēthargia* (forgetfulness).

5. **tractable**—D: Docile; easily handled, managed or controlled; as, a *tractable* pony. Latin *tractare* (to handle, treat).

6. **nurture**—C: To nourish; care for or support during the growth period; foster; as, to *nurture* a new business. Latin *nutrire*.

7. **inchoate**—D: Incomplete; only recently begun; as, an *inchoate* plan to lower mortgage rates. Latin *inchoare* (to begin).

8. **satiate**—A: To glut; surfeit; have so much of something as to kill interest or desire; as, to *satiate* oneself with sweets. Latin *satiare* (to sate, overfill).

9. **obsession**—B: Persistent, compulsive preoccupation with an idea or feeling; as, an *obsession* with one's health. Latin *obsidere* (to beset).

10. **appease**—C: To placate; pacify; conciliate; as, to *appease* an aggressor by surrendering territory. Old French *apaisier*, from *paix* (peace).

11. **prognosis**—B: Forecast of the probable course of an illness; as, an encouraging *prognosis*. Greek *prognosis* (foreknowledge).

12. **frenetic**—A: Frantic; frenzied; hectic; as, a *frenetic* political campaign. Greek *phrenitis* (brain fever).

13. **tenable**—D: Defensible; capable of being held or defended; as, a *tenable* position. Latin *tenere*, (to hold).

14. **aperture**—B: Opening; open space; hole; gap; slit; specifically, the lens opening of a camera. Latin *aperire*, (to open).

15. **eccentric**—C: Unconventional; odd; differing from accepted appearance or behavior; as, an *eccentric* dresser. Greek *ekkentros* (out of the center).

16. **precocious**—A: Unusually mature for one's age; developed earlier than normal; as, a *precocious* child. Latin *praecoquere* (to ripen before the time).

17. **graphic**—B: Vivid; sharply outlined; described with pictorial effect; as, a *graphic* newspaper story. Greek *graphikos*, from *graphein* (to write).

18. **terrestrial**—D: Earthly; relating to land as distinct from air or water; as, *terrestrial* resources. Latin *terrestris*, from *terra* (earth).

19. **paroxysm**—A: Spasm; fit; sudden violent outburst; as, a *paroxysm* of coughing. Greek *paroxysmos*, from *paroxyncin* (to stimulate).

20.   **erosion**—C: Deterioration; progressive destruction by wearing away; as, the *erosion* of money by inflation. Latin *erodere* (to eat away).

VOCABULARY RATINGS

20—18 correct ....master (exceptional)
17—13 correct .... player (excellent)
12—9 correct ....novice (good)

It's A Pig World Out There

By PHYLLIS DEMONG

Fallowing are 13 sty-lish pigtures from an imporkant new book—not just another sowl-scratching gehography but an epig that leaps over international boarders—north, sows, east and west. It's for pig-pong players, pigsilated oinkles and aunts, gruntfathers and gruntmothers, gruntchildren . . . for all "snout-hearted men and true." Read this pigliography and go hog-wild.

DOROTHY PORKER

CUPIG

FRANKENSWINE

SOWS PAW

JHOGGERS

ULYSSES S. GRUNT

THE GABOARS

THE
BAY
OF
PIGS

BOY SNOUTS

SWINE LAKE

PIGASUS

SOWSED

SOW-WESTER

Word Power Test No. 5

English From South of the Border

By PETER FUNK

The English language has always been hospitable to foreign words. For example, each of the "immigrants" in this test comes from Spain or Latin America. Yet this is only a small sampling, for there are many other Spanish words in everyday English use—common words such as *poncho, siesta, mustang, pinto, mañana.* In the test below, choose the word or phrase you believe is *nearest in meaning* to the key word. Answers appear after this test.

1. **wrangler** (rang′ gler)—A: lawman. B: cowboy. C: inventor. D: arbitrator.
2. **lariat** (lăr ē it)—A: hat band. B: saddle thong. C: leather choker. D: lasso.
3. **arroyo** (a roi′ ō)—A: dry gulch. B: spur. C: colorful sash. D: dignity.
4. **hacienda** (ha sē en′ da)—A: ranch. B: grape arbor. C: grove. D: porch.
5. **mantilla** (man tē′ a)—A: scarf. B: insect. C: jewelry. D: heavy cape.

41

6. **sierra** (sē ĕr′ a)—A: mountain range. B: monastery. C: sweeping view. D: parched plain.

7. **El Dorado** (el dō rah′ dō)—A: euphoric state. B: place of wealth and opportunity. C: great leader. D: ideal of national glory.

8. **machismo** (mah chēz′ mō)—A: exaggerated masculinity. B: arrogance. C: good looks. D: pique.

9. **guerrilla** (gĕ rĭl′ a)—A: jungle animal. B: outcast. C: scoundrel. D: irregular fighter.

10. **incommunicado** (in kuh mū nĭ kah′ dō)—A: close-mouthed. B: disguised. C: irreconcilable. D: without means of communication.

11. **junta** (hōōn′ ta: jŭn′ ta)—A: emergency session. B: political excursion. C: irresistible force. D: political clique.

12. **peccadillo** (pĕk ă dĭl′ ō)—A: musical instrument. B: fussiness. C: bullfighter's lance. D: slight fault.

13. **embargo** (em bar′ go)—A: license. B: freight. C: tax. D: prohibition.

14. **fiesta** (fē ĕs′ ta)—A: puzzle. B: joy. C: nap. D: festival.

15. **peon** (pē′ ŏn)—A: food. B: clothing. C: money. D: unskilled laborer.

16. **armada** (ar mah′ da)—A: clothes cabinet. B: fleet of warships. C: throng of people. D: lush valley.

17. **loco** (lō′ kō)—A: humorous. B: erratic. C: insane. D: thoughtful.

18. **pronto** (prahn′ tō)—A: precisely. B: languidly. C: quickly. D: urgently.

19. **escapade** (es′ kă pād)—A: mischievous prank. B: close call. C: surprise raid. D: tall tale.

20. **bonanza** (buh nan′ za)—A: fish fry. B: windfall. C: blessing. D: dessert.

ANSWERS

1. **wrangler**—B: A North American cowboy; herder of livestock. From the last syllables of the American Spanish *caballerango* (groom), from *caballero* (horseman).

2. **lariat**—D: Lasso; rope with sliding noose to catch livestock; a line to tether grazing animals. Spanish *la* (the) and *reata* (rope).

3. **arroyo**—A: Gully or dry stream bed; ravine; creek. Spanish from Latin *arrugia* (mineshaft).

4. **hacienda**—A: Ranch; large estate; main ranch house. Old Spanish *facienda* (employment, estate).

5. **mantilla**—A: Light, ornamental scarf worn over the head and shoulders. Diminutive of Spanish *manta* (cloth, blanket).

6. **sierra**—A: Mountain range rising in peaks resembling the teeth of a saw; as, the *Sierra* Madre in Mexico. Spanish for "saw."

7. **El Dorado**—B: Any place thought to have unusual wealth and opportunity. From a fabled South American city sought by 16th-century explorers. Spanish for "the gilded one."

8. **machismo**—A: Pronounced or exaggerated masculinity: as, "the *machismo* of TV cop Kojak." Mexican Spanish *macho* (virile man) from Latin *masculus* (manly).

9. **guerrilla**—D: Irregular fighter, specializing in ambushes, surprise raids and sabotage behind the lines. Spanish for "little war."

10. **incommunicado**—D: Without any means of communication; as, "The hostages were held *incommunicado*."

11. **junta**—D: Political clique: group ruling a country after seizing power by force; as, a military *junta*.

12. **peccadillo**—D: Slight or trifling fault; minor sin; as, "He was guilty of one *peccadillo:* smoking cigars before breakfast."

13. **embargo**—D: An official prohibition or restriction of foreign trade: as, "We must plan a defense against another oil *embargo*." Spanish *embargar* (to arrest, embargo).

14. **fiesta**—D: Any festivity, celebration, holiday. A religious festival in Spain and Latin America: as, "The running of the bulls is the highlight of the *fiesta* in Pamplona."

15. **peon**—D: Unskilled laborer; derogatory term for someone in an inferior position; person working off a debt. Spanish from Medieval Latin *pedo* (foot soldier).

16. **armada**—B: Fleet of warships; large group of vehicles, airplanes, etc.; as, an *armada* of assault landing craft. Spanish from Medieval Latin *armata* (army, fleet).

17. **loco**—C: Slang term meaning insane, demented or mentally disoriented; as, "The cowboy said the flies were driving him *loco*."

18. **pronto**—C: Slang for quickly, promptly, at once, imme-

diately: as, "Let's get out of here *pronto*."

19. **escapade**—A: Mischievous prank; carefree or reckless adventure; as, a college *escapade*. Adaptation of Spanish *escapada* (escape).

20. **bonanza**—B: Windfall; source of wealth or profits; as, "The uranium discovery yielded a *bonanza*." Spanish for "fair weather," thus, figuratively, prosperity or success.

VOCABULARY RATINGS

20—18 correct .... master (exceptional)
17—13 correct .... player (excellent)
12—9 correct .... novice (good)

In (Reverent, Loving, Thankful) Praise of Books!

By JOAN MILLS

My teacher told my mother that I seemed to be tracing the words in my reader with my nose. And so, a few days later, I arrived at my classroom walking wobbly because the ground wasn't where it had been, and proud because now I wasn't just the littlest kid in school. I was the littlest kid with spectacles! Grandly through the door I went, stunning everybody; but then, I'd known I would.

The entire first grade crowded near, hollering for turns; grabby little boys in knickers and homemade haircuts, jealous little girls wearing butterfly bows and starched dresses. Miss Browne paused in distributing that morning's construction paper and paste, and smiled at the beamishness of me.

My new glasses went from hand to hand, from one befuddled set of eyes to the next. When they were returned, I thought them much improved by fingerprints, a loosened fit and the honor of it all. Carefully then, I hooked them over my ears, ceremoniously opened my reader, and held it at a comfortable distance. There on the page, still and crisp and bright, lay words of lovely legibility.

Not that I could read much. We were only up to *cat, hat, bat, mat* and *rat.* But I loved reading anyway. I loved it even when it was hard, because I so loved books. I liked the heft of a book, grownup and significant. My senses faintly reeled at the scent of paper, printer's ink and glue. There was something profoundly satisfying to the shapes of letters and the neatness of words laid out exactly so upon the pages.

When I had been smaller yet, sitting tight against my mother while she read to me, I'd wondered how the inked words kept bedtime stories the same in every telling, the way I wanted them to be. I would whisper along with my mother's voice and shiver in the right places. Maybe, I thought, words held stories inside books like thumbtacks, so they couldn't slide around— which is how it is, actually; thoughts and images pinned in place.

So in school I worked eagerly onward from *cat* and *rat* toward high adventure. I caught my breath with excitement when I came upon big words like *goblins* or *gingerbread,* and hurried to read more.

When at last I was reading real stories, the magical properties of words seemed even greater than before. Sometimes I held a book at arm's length, wanting to see what it was really made of. Printed paper, bound into covers! How could anything so flat and black and white fill my head and dizzy my heart? How, just by my eyes seeing words, could I see clear visions of what I had never seen? Hear marching bands, when silence filled the room?

Pulling the book closer, I leaned to study words one by one. In my speller, the same words had no life. Here, arranged in different order, no more than that, they swept me into miracles. *Why?* How could that be?

Marveling, certain of magic, I followed the tracery of words into a story, and was transported from where I sat. I felt a deep tremor of awe and anticipation each time I opened a new book and smoothed the first page in a gesture of beginning. Why such certainty of joy? Not every book was wonderful, surely. I'd read a few that weren't. But this one might be! And it would be different from any other I had read, some way, somehow.

In those days, life for me, as for all children, was vivid, full and felt. There was everything to see, learn, do, react to, imagine. Twirling in my swing, I set the backyard to spinning in wild circles about me. I looked into the heightened colors of summertime and wondered if there were more colors yet— unknown to me, but there. In the moon-shadowed room where I slept, I worried about ghosts, arithmetic, and pleasing my parents. I knew myself to be small, and wished otherwise.

The habit of reading came as naturally to my childhood as all of these; as spontaneously as make-believe or the seasons. In the crotched branches of a bent apple tree, I read, and waited for a baby robin to burst his blue shell. I read in the attic, listening to the enclosing sound of rain, or out in the old packing box that served me for playhouse, cave and castle.

I read along with breakfast, wiggling my loose tooth; I read after supper, while my parents listened to the radio to hear what Mr. Roosevelt was up to. I read on the trolley car, all the way to my music lesson. Finally, in a bed lumpy with literature, I fell asleep as if among friends. The busiest of my days completed themselves with happy endings.

So I became a reader early; and I've been bookish ever since. The pleasure I find in books has never worn away, though my grownup days are as eventful, dutiful and various as any I spent when I was a child. Now it's meetings, people, work and taxes. The weeds, the wash; this to paint and that to mend. It's emergencies and holidays and the telephone ringing. I drive the freeways, pedal my bike down quiet avenues, run for buses, chase after my very thoughts.

Life is a *lot,* I think sometimes. But here, on my coffee table, is a book set down beside a bowl of red and yellow apples. It is as pleasant an invitation to peacefulness and philosophy as any I know.

Whatever my life may hold—or lack—there is always an orderly mind for me to consult when my own seems less than sensible. Reading, I am spared a great deal of loneliness, ineptness and loss of faith. My private hours are fulfilled by admiration and compassion for the varieties of human experience. The world seems all the more precious to me for knowing something of its origins, fragility, beauty, mystery, and locus in sprawling infinity. I laugh, which we all need. And on I go.

Like the green plants banked in my window and the familiar dishes set out on the table, books express and furnish my life. I like them where I can see them, ranged on shelves. They are friendly presences, beautiful and agreeable. And there's always a new one to take into hand.

That's the joy of it—that, and the ever-refreshed anticipatory tremor that I feel as purely as when I was very young. I push my glasses firmly on my nose, the habit of many years; settle myself, and turn to the first page. There is something fresh and unguessed-at here for me to know—and I'm about to find it out!

Word Power Test No. 6

Talk to the Animals

By PETER FUNK

Among the creatures lurking behind the 20 words below you will find cranes, cattle, oxen, goats, whales and even worms. Some are obvious, some camouflaged. Yet each has given one or another of its traits to these nouns, adjectives and verbs. Pick the word or phrase *nearest in meaning* to the key word. Check your results at the end of this test.

1. **pedigree** (ped′ uh grē)—A: ancestral line. B: warrant. C: diploma. D: public record.
2. **apian** (āp′ ĭ an)—concerning A: an ape. B: a sloth. C: a bee. D: a gazelle.
3. **pecuniary** (pē kū′ nē ĕr e)—having to do with A: money. B: architecture. C: warfare. D: indolence.
4. **cornucopia** (kor nuh kō′ pĭ a)—A: crown of flowers. B: haystack. C: carved molding. D: horn-shaped container.
5. **exuberant** (ĭg zoo′ ber ant)—A: passionate. B: reckless. C: joyously unrestrained. D: grandiose.

6. **behemoth** (be hē′ moth)—A: stinging insect. B: huge beast. C: holiday mood. D: mythological creature.

7. **preen**—A: to stitch. B: tidy oneself up. C: exaggerate. D: strut.

8. **caper**—A: antic. B: implement. C: lamp. D: party.

9. **lionize**—A: to devour. B: assess. C: treat as a celebrity. D: neglect.

10. **harangue** (hă rang′)—A: tirade. B: poem. C: vessel. D: cactus.

11. **canard** (kă nard′)—A: false story. B: trite remark. C: proverb. D: small bucket.

12. **zodiacal** (zō dī′ ah k'l)—having to do with A: zoos. B: machinery. C: ghosts. D: constellations.

13. **congregate** (con′ gre gate)—A: to assemble. B: accumulate. C: summon. D: scatter.

14. **leviathan** (le vī′ uh thun)—something A: thin. B: small. C: gigantic. D: clumsy.

15. **ferret** (fĕr′ it)—A: to conceal. B: weigh. C: disperse. D: search.

16. **vermin**—A: welcome guests. B: fur wraps. C: true accounts. D: objectionable pests.

17. **vulpine** (vŭl′ pin)—A: revolting. B: lecherous. C: fiery. D: crafty.

18. **bugbear**—A: hoax. B: oddment. C: cause of anxiety. D: small animal.

19. **halcyon** (hal′ sē un)—A: turbulent. B: shimmering. C: exhausting. D: calm.

20. **gadfly**—A: a gossip. B: restless person. C: dullard. D: annoying person.

ANSWERS

1. **pedigree**—A: Ancestral line; lineage. From Middle French *pié de grue* (foot of crane), which is what the diagram marks linking one generation to the next resemble.

2. **apian**—C: Concerning a bee, or bees. "A beeline is an *apian* shortcut." Latin *apis* (bee).

3. **pecuniary**—A: Having to do with money. Latin *pecus* (cattle), the earliest form of measurable wealth.

4. **cornucopia**—D: Horn-shaped container overflowing with

food and flowers, symbolizing prosperity. Latin *cornu* (horn) and *copia* (plenty).

5. **exuberant**—C: Joyously unrestrained and enthusiastic; vivacious. In the eyes of the ancient Romans, an *exuberant* person figuratively resembled "overflowing udders." Latin *exuberare* (to be very fruitful) from *ex* (out) and *uber* (udder).

6. **behemoth**—B: Huge beast, as in Job 40: 15–24, "Behold now *behemoth*, which I have made with thee; he eateth grass as an ox." Hebrew.

7. **preen**—B: We *preen* when, from vanity, we tidy up the way we look in too fussy a manner. From Middle English *prunen*, referring to a bird trimming and dressing its feathers.

8. **caper**—A: Antic; prank. "Kidnapping an opponent's mascot is a typical undergraduate *caper*." From Latin *capreolus* (wild goat).

9. **lionize**—C: To treat as a celebrity. From Old French *leon*, which became English "lion."

10. **harangue**—A: Tirade; bombastic speech. "In a 26-city speaking tour, the politician repeated the same long *harangue*." From Old Italian *aringo* (a public horse-race ring) where speeches were made.

11. **canard**—A: A false story, usually one spread by the media; as, "The report of price-fixing was a *canard*." French *canard* (duck) from *vendre des canards à moitié* (to sell half a duck; hence, swindle).

12. **zodiacal**—D: Having to do with constellations. "Those born in the first half of March have Pisces, the fishes, as their *zodiacal* sign." Greek *zodiakos kyklos* (circle of animals).

13. **congregate**—A: To assemble; come together. "Enthusiastic fans *congregate* around the singer." Latin *congregare* from *com-* (together) and *grex* (a flock of animals).

14. **leviathan**—C: Something gigantic; as, "A supertanker is a *leviathan* of the sea." Hebrew *liwyathan* (large Biblical sea creature—a huge crocodile or whale).

15. **ferret**—D: To search around; hunt; as, "Intelligence services tried to *ferret* out the identity of the spy." The weasel-like *ferret* derives its name from the Latin *fur* (thief).

16. **vermin**—D: Pests, such as lice or rats. "The houses are dilapidated, ill-heated, *vermin*-infested." Latin *vermis* (worm).

17. **vulpine**—D: A *vulpine* merchant is crafty or sly in the

manner of a fox. Latin *vulpes* (fox).

18. **bugbear**—C: Whatever causes seemingly needless or excessive anxiety or fear; as, "The *bugbear* of a tax audit gave him concern." Middle English *bugge* (hobgoblin) and bear.

19. **halcyon**—D: *Halcyon* days are calm, idyllic times. From Greek *halkyon*, a mythological bird that nested at sea, calming wind and waves.

20. **gadfly**—D: Annoying fly. Therefore, any annoying person; one who rouses others from complacency by provocative criticism. Old Norse *gaddr* (spike, sting) and fly.

VOCABULARY RATINGS

20—18 correct ....master (exceptional)
17—13 correct .... player (excellent)
12—9 correct ....novice (good)

Murder and the Mother Tongue

By WALLACE CARROLL

I rise to speak of murder. "Murder most foul, strange and unnatural," as the ghost in *Hamlet* called it. Or, to use the more precise words of Professor Henry Higgins in *My Fair Lady* "the cold-blooded murder of the English tongue."

This cold-blooded murder is committed with impunity day in and day out, and each one of us is at least an accomplice. The language of our fathers is mauled in the public schools, butchered in the universities, mangled on Madison Avenue, flayed in the musty halls of the bureaucracy and tortured without mercy on 1000 copy desks.

Because of our brutality and neglect, the English that is our heritage from Shakespeare, from Shelley and Keats, from Dickens and Thackeray and Kipling—this English is now on its way to the limbo of dead languages. Certainly, the language has changed more in the past ten years than in the previous 100. And the change has been entirely for the worse.

This debasement of English as we have known it should concern everyone, for the English language is one of our great natural resources. Yet we are now polluting this priceless resource as senselessly as we have polluted the air and lakes and streams, and the consequences for the American people could be as grave.

The assault on the language begins in the schools. We all know how Abraham Lincoln learned to read, lying on the floor of a log cabin, a candle at his elbow, puzzling out the words in an old Bible. Now, if Lincoln had enjoyed the advantages of our present-day schooling, he would never have discovered the strength and beauty of the language in this way. For Abe would have learned, not to read, but to "acquire a reading skill," a curious term that suggests what a plumber's apprentice goes through in acquiring a plumbing skill. The teacher, whose courses in education had taught that reading is a hard, tedious, mechanical process, would have conveyed the same feeling to the boy. And so Lincoln might have become an adequate plumber, but he certainly would not have written the Gettysburg Address.

Of course, the term "reading skills" is only the most obvious symptom of a linguistic blight that someone has called "Educanto." A teacher who has mastered Educanto can rattle off such expressions as "learner-centered merged curriculum" and "empirically validated learning package," and assure you that "underachievers and students who have suffered environmental deprivation can be helped by differentiated staffing and elaborated modes of conceptual visualization."

In a spirit of mercy I shall skip what is done to the language Madison Avenue-wise and business-wise, and proceed directly to the apex of government in Washington.

Here we discover that the President doesn't make a choice or decision: he "exercises his options." He doesn't send a message to the Russians: he "initiates a dialogue"—and "hopefully" it's a "meaningful dialogue." He doesn't simply try something new: he "introduces innovative techniques."

Those of us who write and edit the news should be, above all, the protectors of the public against this kind of barbarism. But what do we do? We not only pass along to the reader the Educanto, the gobbledygook and the federalese; we even add some nifty little touches of our own. Thus the resourceful reporter uncovers "meaningful decisions" and "meaningful dialogues" all over the landscape, while editorial writers assure us that these meaningful dialogues are adding "new dimensions" to our "pluralistic society."

Why should I care so much about this? Why should *anyone* care?

Well, as I said earlier, the English language is one of our great natural resources. At least twice during my lifetime I have seen the English-speaking nations raised from despair and defeat almost by the power of the language alone.

The first time was during the Great Depression. It is hard to realize today how low our people had fallen. The farmer was driven from his farm. The worker was sent home from the factory. Fathers scrounged in garbage cans. Mothers starved themselves to feed their children. Until then, America had always gone confidently forward. Was this the end of the American dream?

Then we heard on the radio the voice—the unforgettable voice—of Franklin Roosevelt:

"The only thing we have to fear is fear itself."

As he spoke, people began to hope again. Go back to the history of those days and read the words of Roosevelt. Easy English words. Simple, declarative English sentences.

Then go back to the year 1940, when Hitler's armies were driving the French and British forces back across France, and Britain faced imminent invasion. Then the British people heard the words of Winston Churchill:

"I have nothing to offer but blood, toil, tears and sweat."

Blood, toil, tears and sweat—four bleak, one-syllable, Old English words. Only a great leader would have dared to make such a promise—and the British people suddenly knew they had such a leader.

And when Churchill turned to America for help, note that he did not say: "Supply us with the necessary inputs of relevant equipment, and we shall implement the program and accomplish its objectives." No. He said:

"Give us the tools, and we will finish the job."

And, across the Atlantic, Roosevelt heard him and spoke this simple analogy to the American people:

"Suppose my neighbor's home catches fire, and I have a length of garden hose. If he can take my garden hose and connect it up with his hydrant, I may help him put out his fires. Now, what do I do? I don't say to him before that operation, 'Neighbor, my garden hose cost me $15, you have to pay me $15 for it.' I don't want $15; I want my garden hose back after the fire is over."

With such plain backyard talk, Lend-Lease was born, Britain was saved, and America gained time to arm for war.

My friends, the English language has stood us in good stead. And never doubt for a moment that we shall need it again in all its power and nobility.

Let us *not* allow the latter-day barbarians to rob us of this birthright. Rather, taking our watchword from Winston Churchill, let us resolve today:

We shall fight them in the school rooms, we shall fight them on the campuses, we shall fight them in the clammy corridors of the bureaucracy, we shall fight them at their mikes and at their typewriters. And when we win—as win we shall—we shall bury them in the rubble of their own jargon. Because, Lord knows, they deserve nothing better.

IT PAYS TO ENRICH YOUR WORD POWER ®

Word Power Test No. 7

And Now for the Latest News

By PETER FUNK

In this list of words frequently encountered in the news, check the word or phrase you believe is *nearest in meaning* to the key word. Results appear after this test.

1. **hegemony** (hĕ jem′ o nē)—A: government by the few. B: mass migration. C: self-governing state. D: dominance.
2. **imperialism** (im pēr′ ĭ al iz′m)—A: empire-building. B: arrogance. C: aristocratic rule. D: tyranny.
3. **plebiscite** (pleb′ ĭ sīt)—A: militant youth. B: common people. C: minority representation. D: direct popular vote.
4. **reclamation** (rek la mā′ shun)—A: official announcement. B: restoration. C: demand. D: proposal.
5. **abdicate** (ab′ dĭ kāt)—A: to abolish. B: plead for. C: censure. D: renounce.
6. **bondage** (bon′ dij)—A: security. B: debt. C: slavery. D: contract.
7. **legation** (lĕ gā′ shun)—A: lawsuit. B: diplomatic mission. C: orderly process. D: lawmaking.

8. **repatriate** (re pā′ trĭ ăt)—A: to return home. B: colonize. C: brainwash. D: repay.

9. **détente** (dā tahnt′)—A: collusion. B: stalemate. C: easing. D: delay.

10. **decelerate** (dē sel′ er āt)—A: to destroy. B: slow. C: isolate. D: free.

11. **caliph** (kā′ lif)—A: guide. B: secret group. C: Muslim leader. D: prophet.

12. **conditional** (kon dish′ un al)—A: practical. B: plausible. C: special. D: contingent.

13. **impose** (im pōz′)—A: to force upon. B: shock. C: influence. D: upset.

14. **option** (op′ shun)—A: substitute. B: choice. C: consent. D: wish.

15. **annex** (a neks′)—A: to take control of. B: subordinate. C: align. D: overrun.

16. **oligarchy** (ol′ ĭ gar kē)—A: dictatorship. B: rule by many. C: chaos. D: government by a few.

17. **commingle** (kŏ ming′ g′l)—A: to confuse. B: adulterate. C: combine. D: make whole.

18. **constitutional** (kon stĭ tū′ shun al)—A: elective. B: lawful. C: supreme. D: ancient.

19. **media** (mē′ dĭ a)—A: average. B: marketing. C: consensus. D: means of dispensing information.

20. **chronic** (krŏn′ ik)—A: continuous. B: acute. C: widespread. D: cranky.

ANSWERS

1. **hegemony**—D: Dominance or preponderant influence of one nation over others; as, a spreading Soviet *hegemony*. Greek *hegemon* (leader).

2. **imperialism**—A: Empire-building; extension of a nation's power and dominion by gaining territorial, political or economic control over other nations. Latin *imperium* (empire).

3. **plebiscite**—D: Direct vote of the people of a country or district on an important public question. Latin *plebi scitum* (decree of the people).

4. **reclamation**—B: Restoration to a useful condition; as, the *reclamation* of barren, unproductive land. Latin *reclamare* (to cry out against).

5.   **abdicate**—D: To renounce; relinquish formally; as, to *abdicate* leadership. Latin *abdicare*.

6.   **bondage**—C: Slavery; serfdom; as, political prisoners held in *bondage*. Middle English *bonde* (serf).

7.   **legation**—B: Diplomatic mission headed by a minister; also, the minister's official residence and office. Latin *legare* (to delegate).

8.   **repatriate**—A: To return to the country of origin; as, to *repatriate* refugees. Latin *repatriare* (to go back to one's country).

9.   **détente**—C: Easing of tensions between nations; as, a precarious *détente* between the United States and Soviet Russia. Middle French *destendre* (to slacken).

10. **decelerate**—B: To slow down; decrease the speed of; retard; as, to *decelerate* inflation. Latin *de-* (from) and *celerare* (to hasten).

11. **caliph**—C: Muslim leader; originally, a successor of Mohammed. Arabic *khalifah,* from *khalafa* (to succeed).

12. **conditional**—D: Contingent or dependent on something else; limited by conditions; as, a *conditional* contract. Latin *condicere* (to agree).

13. **impose**—A: To force upon; levy; as, to *impose* a tax. Latin *imponcre* (to put or place upon).

14. **option**—B: Choice; freedom to choose between alternatives; as, to offer *options* for settling a claim. Latin *optio* (free choice).

15. **annex**—A: To take control or possession of; assume jurisdiction over; as, to *annex* adjoining territory. Latin *annectere* (to bind to).

16. **oligarchy**—D: Government by a few; as, China's imperturbable *oligarchy*. Greek *oligarchia* from *oligos* (few) and *archein* (to rule).

17. **commingle**—C: To combine; mix; mingle; blend; as, to force ethnically disparate tribes to *commingle*. Latin *commiscere* (to mix together).

18. **constitutional**—B: Lawful; consistent with the fundamental principles established by the constitution of a state or society; as, a citizen's *constitutional* rights. Latin *constituere* (to set up, constitute).

19. **media**—D: Means of dispensing information or news; channels of communication; as, an event given wide coverage by the *media*. Plural of Latin *medium*.

20. **chronic**—A: Continuous; constant; prolonged; recurring periodically; as, *chronic* warfare. Greek *chronikos*, from *chronos* (time).

VOCABULARY RATINGS

20—18 correct ....master (exceptional)
17—13 correct .... player (excellent)
12—9 correct ....novice (good)

How's That Again?

Condensed from
The COLUMBIA JOURNALISM REVIEW

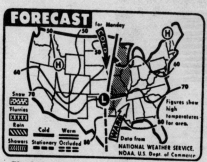

Shaded parts of map locate areas occupied by Israel since 1967.

MILWAUKEE *SENTINEL.*
10/31/77

Missionary risked dysentery and bigamy in eight day trip to Nigerian villages

GAINESVILLE, GA., *TIMES.* 10/14/77

That routine has often been broken by Vance's frequent travel, a duty he dislikes, although he is beginning to sleep better aboard the department's aircraft. His demanding tasks have kept him away from his family, which includes four daughters and a son, far more than he would like.

TIME. 4/24/78

**Shoot kids
to halt flu,
study says**

ORLANDO *SENTINEL STAR.*
3/16/78

JOHNNY CASH and his wife, June Carter, one of country music's favorite couples

FORT MYERS, FLA.
NEWS-PRESS
2/19/78

Signature ship

A sailor applies the final touch to America's most famous signature on the Navy's newest destroyer, being readied for commissioning ceremonies Saturday at Ingalls Shipbuilding yard in Pascagoula, Miss. (UPI)

ELYRIA, OHIO.
CHRONICLE-TELEGRAM
3/6/79

City May Impose Mandatory Time For Prostitution

TAMPA *TRIBUNE*.
8/7/79

Indian Ocean talks

CLEVELAND *PLAIN DEALER*.
10/5/77

President Jimmy Carter and Soviet President Leonid Brezhnev are all smiles as they meet the first time since they boarded the vessel and discovered bails of marijuana.

SAN JUAN, PUERTO RICO.
STAR 6/16/79

Two Soviet ships collide, one dies

BLACKFOOT, IDAHO. *NEWS.* 11/1/79

Word Power Test No. 8

Double-headers

By PETER FUNK

Each of the ten words below has at least two different meanings. Check the word or phrase you believe is *nearest in meaning* to the key word. Answers appear after this test.

1. **address** (a drěs')—A: to make amends. B: soothe. C: mark directions for delivery on. D: bring out.
2. **address**—A: to challenge. B: advise. C: confront. D: apply one's efforts to.
3. **dispense** (dis pens')—A: to scatter. B: deal out. C: reject. D: disregard.
4. **dispense**—A: to do without. B: denote. C: lose. D: dishonor.
5. **submit** (sub mit')—A: to consider. B: evade. C: yield. D: agree.
6. **submit**—A: to expose. B: offer. C: rebel. D: incite.
7. **access** (ak' ses)—A: improvement. B: aid. C: admittance or passage. D: summons.
8. **access**—A: outburst. B: acceptance. C: hope. D: vanity.

9. **assume** (a sūm′)—A: to state with authority. B: gather. C: assist. D: take for granted.
10. **assume**—A: to bind or limit. B: adopt. C: ensure. D: strive.
11. **retainer** (re tān′ er)—A: delay. B: secret. C: detention in custody. D: fee.
12. **retainer**—A: servant. B: adviser. C: bill. D: deputy.
13. **prone** (prōn)—A: relaxed. B: inclined. C: quick. D: humble.
14. **prone**—A: haughty. B: exhausted. C: ashamed. D: prostrate.
15. **regard** (re gard′)—A: to thank. B: worry. C: look at. D: compliment.
16. **regard**—A: to heed. B: be sorry for. C: doubt. D: flatter.
17. **expedition** (eks pe dish′ un)—A: adventure. B: experience. C: disbursement. D: journey for a specific purpose.
18. **expedition**—A: accuracy. B: intelligence. C: speed. D: grace.
19. **maintain** (mān tān′)—A: to keep in condition. B: cure. C: furnish. D: raise.
20. **maintain**—A: to master. B: affirm. C: defeat. D: respect.

ANSWERS

1. **address**—C: To mark directions for delivery on; as, to *address* a letter. Middle French *addresser* (to arrange).
2. **address**—D: To apply one's efforts or energy to; direct one's attention to; as, to *address* (oneself to) the reporter's question.
3. **dispense**—B: To deal out in portions; distribute; as, to *dispense* rations. Latin *dispendere* (to weigh out).
4. **dispense**—A: To do without; give up; forgo; as, to *dispense* with luxuries.
5. **submit**—C: To yield to governance or authority; defer to another's wish or opinion; as, to *submit* to authoritarian rule. Latin *submittere*.
6. **submit**—B: To offer; present; make available; as, to *submit* documentary evidence.
7. **access**—C: Admittance or passage; permission or freedom to enter, pass to and from, or to make use of; as, to have ready *access* to the records. Latin *accedere* (to approach).

8.   **access**—A: Outburst; fit of intense feeling; as, an *access* of fury.

9.   **assume**—D: To take for granted; suppose; as, to *assume* the truth of a statement. Latin *assumere* (to take to oneself).

10.   **assume**—B: To adopt; take to or upon oneself; take in appearance only; feign; as, to *assume* an uncharacteristic detachment.

11.   **retainer**—D: Fee paid (often in advance) to secure professional services, as of a lawyer. Latin *retinere* (to hold back, keep).

12.   **retainer**—A: Servant, especially one attached to a person of rank or to a household; as, a royal *retainer*.

13.   **prone**—B: Inclined; having a tendency or inclination; disposed; as, *prone* to laughter. Latin *pronus* (bent forward, tending).

14.   **prone**—D: Lying flat or prostrate, especially face downward; as, *prone* on the pavement.

15.   **regard**—C: To look at attentively; watch; as, to *regard* the witness closely. Old French *regarder* (to look back at).

16.   **regard**—A: To heed; pay attention to; respect; show consideration for; as, to *regard* the rights of the minority.

17.   **expedition**—D: Journey for a specific purpose; as, an archeological *expedition*. Latin *expedire* (to set free, make ready).

18.   **expedition**—C: Speed; efficient promptness; dispatch; as, a trial jury picked with remarkable *expedition*.

19.   **maintain**—A: To keep in condition; preserve; sustain; uphold; defend; as, to *maintain* the rule of law. Latin *manu tenere* (to hold in the hand).

20.   **maintain**—B: To affirm in argument; assert; as, to *maintain* one's innocence of wrongdoing.

VOCABULARY RATINGS

20—18 correct .... master (exceptional)
17—13 correct .... player (excellent)
12—9 correct .... novice (good)

"The English: How She Is Talked"

By H. ALLEN SMITH

I'm quite certain that Mrs. Mardsley was paved with good intentions when she gave me the little book. The moment she found out I was contemplating an Italian journey, she insisted that I have it.

She hastened to explain that this was no ordinary language guidebook of the type customarily carried by American tourists. It was a guide written for Italians, a *Manuale di Conversazione Italiano-Inglese* or, in my own smooth translation, "The English: How She Is Talked."

"With this little volume," Mrs. Mardsley told me, "you will learn to talk about the things that Italians talk about among themselves."

I flipped open the book, and my eye fell on this exchange:

"What was the loud noise?"

"Oh, nothing. Just an explosion."

I looked at Mrs. Mardsley, who said, "Not there. Let me show you how. Just open it at random."

Pretending continental insouciance, I turned a few leaves

and, using the hatpin system of picking horses, jabbed my finger at the righthand page. It said: *"Non potete insegnare alla nonna a bere le nova.* Don't try to teach your grandmother to suck eggs."

Mrs. Mardsley bent over and inspected the lines and then scowled at me, as if *I* had written them.

"How about *that?*" I said. "Am I going around the streets of Rome and Venice and Naples saying *that* to the Italian people?"

"Please," she protested. "Turn to some place in the middle—hotels and railroads and the post office." I did, and arrived at a section dealing with signs: "Beware of the dog! Beware of sheep! Beware of pickpockets!" And my eye fell on a startling line: "My collarbones are broken."

I closed my eyes and shook my head briskly and pondered the preoccupations of Italian small talk. A loud noise that was nothing, just an explosion, brought me out of my reflections— it was Mrs. Mardsley urging me to try another section of the little book.

I went to work and quickly discovered that, if I am to enjoy myself to the fullest in Italy, I should be able to convey such light-hearted sentiments as: "I am cold. I am hot. I am hungry. I am tired. I am ill. Can you help me? It was not my fault. I cannot find my hotel. I have lost my friends.· I forgot my money. I have lost my keys. I have missed the train. They are bothering me. Go away. I have been robbed. Where is the Lost and Found desk? That razor scratches. No, I part my hair on the other side."

I was getting into a state of nerves. It had been my aim to *noleggiare automobili* in Italy and let them put me in the driver's seat, so I feverishly slipped to the appropriate section and found, "Excuse me, I was confused by the traffic; I am a stranger here," quickly followed by the question, "How much is the fine?" Same as everywhere else—you can't win. And then: "My tire has collapsed. It is a slow leak. My engine skips. There is a grinding. There is a diminution of power. It stops. You must change the bush of the engine, register the tappets." A bit further on, I found: "I came in from your left and so I had the precedence. It was your fault."

Maybe, I thought, I had better not rent a car. How about, instead, a nice boat trip in the lovely Adriatic? I hopefully turned to matters *marittime* and there it was, the same dirge, Italian-style: "I am sick. Please show me the quickest way to my cabin. Are you sure we are on course? Where are the pills? Go away." Cruising the Adriatic—*out*.

Remembering my customary concern for my health when traveling, I turned with morbid fascination to the medical section. Pretty soon I was suffering maladies I had never known before, for the spirited *conversazione* went: "I have a pain in my back, in my stomach, in my head, in my kidneys, in some bones. Taxi, be quick! I feel these pains before eating. When riding. When I walk fast. Sitting down. I suffer from headaches, dizziness, nausea, colics of the liver, nettle-rash, *morbillo* (measles) and *orecchioni* (mumps)." I fled right out of that chapter, like a startled gazelle.

By this time I was feeling pretty glum (*sconsolato*). It seemed unreasonable to me that a vacation in sunny Italy should be so fraught with disaster, unprogrammed interruptions such as colics of the liver, unregistered tappets, collarbones cracking in pairs, man-eating sheep and withered grandmothers sitting around sucking eggs.

"It may be," I said to Mrs. Mardsley, "that I'll postpone my trip to Italy."

Then suddenly the truth hit me. The little book was not about Italy at all. The dangers and disasters described were not endemic to Rome or Florence. They were put into print for the benefit of Italians getting ready to travel among *us* . . . in the United States! A great oppression lifted from my spirit, a heady eagerness seized me. I wanted to head out for Italy *immediatamente*. After all, it is good for the soul to get away from one's own kind for a while, away from one's own barber who can't even locate the part in one's hair, from where even *I* can't locate the Lost and Found desk.

IT PAYS TO ENRICH YOUR WORD POWER ®

Word Power Test No. 9

The Declaration of Independence

By PETER FUNK

In 1776 the following 20 words appeared in the Declaration of Independence, a document that altered America's history. Today, their meanings virtually unchanged, these words remain sentinels of our liberties. Check the word or phrase that you believe is *nearest in meaning* to the key word. Answers appear at the end of this test.

1. **dissolve** (dĭ zolv′)—A: to mix. B: cloud. C: terminate. D: abandon.
2. **endow** (en dow′)—A: to approve. B: immobilize. C: embark. D: provide.
3. **obstruct** (ob strukt′)—A: to facilitate. B: close. C: block. D: handicap.
4. **prudence** prōō′ dens)—A: high-mindedness. B: excessive primness. C: lewdness. D: sound judgment.
5. **disposed** (dis pōzd′)—A: inclined toward. B: deprived of. C: spread out. D: tolerated.

71

6. **invariable** (in var′ ĭ ă b′l)—A: similar. B: constant. C: universal. D: usual.

7. **multitude** (mul′ tĭ tūde)—A: immeasurability. B: paucity. C: a great many. D: diversity.

8. **constrain** (kon strān′)—A: to relax. B: overdo. C: moderate. D: compel.

9. **tyranny** (tir′ ă nē)—A: tolerance. B: supra-national government. C: predominance. D: oppressive government.

10. **candid** (kan′ did)—A: quick. B: hidden. C: impartial. D: harsh.

11. **arbitrary** (ar′ bĭ trĕr ē)—A: humble. B: based on one's own notions. C: persistent to a harmful degree. D: selfish.

12. **relinquish** (rē ling′ kwish)—A: to give up. B: enjoy. C: circumscribe. D: take pleasure in.

13. **inestimable** (in es′ tĭ ma b′l)—A: beyond calculation. B: obvious. C: not to be endured. D: inexpensive.

14. **compliance** (kom plī′ ans)—A: yielding to a demand. B: self-satisfaction. C: firm enforcement. D: belief.

15. **endeavor** (en dev′ er)—A: to ignore. B: intend. C: attempt earnestly. D: bring about.

16. **usurpation** (ū sur pā′ shun)—A: revolution. B: utilization. C: disputation. D: unlawful seizure.

17. **magnanimity** (mag nă nim′ ĭ tē)—A: nobility of spirit. B: exaggeration. C: enormous size. D: optimism.

18. **rectitude** (rek′ tĭ tūde)—A: austerity. B: pride. C: honesty. D: inflexibility.

19. **insurrection** (in sŭ rek′ shun)—A: discontent. B: objection. C: revolt. D: disobedience.

20. **redress** (rē dres′)—A: overcoat. B: reprieve. C: reclamation. D: reparation of wrong.

ANSWERS

1. **dissolve**—C: To terminate. "When . . . it becomes necessary for one people to *dissolve* the political bands . . ." Latin *dissolvere* (to loosen).

2. **endow**—D: To provide with a talent or quality; to give property. "*Endowed* by their creator with certain unalienable Rights." Latin *dotare* (to provide with a dowry).

3. **obstruct**—C: To block; impede. "He has *obstructed* the Administration of Justice." Latin *obstruere* (to build against).

4. **prudence**—D: Sound judgment; careful foresight. *"Prudence . . .* will dictate that Governments . . . should not be changed for light and transient causes." Latin *providere* (to look forward to).

5. **disposed**—A: Inclined toward. "Mankind are more *disposed* to suffer . . ." Latin *disponere* (to set in order).

6. **invariable**—B: Constant; not changing or varying. "Pursuing *invariably* the same Object." Late Latin *in* (not) and *variabilis* (changing).

7. **multitude**—C: A great many; large number of persons or things. "He has erected a *multitude* of New Offices." Latin *multitudo*.

8. **constrain**—D: To compel; bring about by force. "The necessity which *constrains* them to alter their former Systems of Government." Also, to restrain; confine. Latin *constringere* (to bind together).

9. **tyranny**—D: Oppressive government; dictatorship. "The establishment of an absolute *Tyranny* over these States." Latin *tyrannus* (absolute ruler).

10. **candid**—C: Impartial; fair. "Let Facts be submitted to a *candid* world." Also, frank; informal. Latin *candere* (to shine).

11. **arbitrary**—B: Based on one's own notions; not guided by law or rules. "Establishing therein an *Arbitrary* government . . ." Latin *arbitrarius*.

12. **relinquish**—A: To give up; surrender; abandon. "Would *relinquish* the right of Representation." Latin *relinquere* (to leave behind).

13. **inestimable**—A: Beyond calculation; invaluable; too great to be measured. "A right *inestimable* to them." Latin *inaestimabilis* (priceless).

14. **compliance**—A: Yielding to a demand; conforming. "Fatiguing them into *compliance* with his measures." Latin *complere* (to fill up).

15. **endeavor**—C: To attempt earnestly; work hard or dutifully with a definite purpose. "He has *endeavoured* to prevent . . ." Middle English *endeveren* (to exert oneself).

16. **usurpation**—D: Unlawful or unjust seizure of property or power. "We have conjured them . . . to disavow these *usurpations.*" Latin *usurpare* (to make use of).

17. **magnanimity**—A: Nobility of spirit; generosity. "We have appealed to their native justice and *magnanimity.*" Latin *magnanimus*, from *magnus* (great) and *animus* (soul).

18. **rectitude**—C: Honesty; uprightness; adhering to rules of right and justice. "Appealing to the Supreme Judge of the world for the *rectitude* of our intentions." Latin *rectus* (straight).

19. **insurrection**—C: Revolt; an uprising, but not yet a full rebellion. "He has excited domestic *insurrections* amongst us." Latin *insurgere* (to rise up).

20. **redress**—D: Reparation of wrong; amends, as for a loss. "We have Petitioned for *Redress* in the most humble terms." Old French *redrecier* (to make straight again).

VOCABULARY RATINGS

20—18 correct ....master (exceptional)
17—13 correct .... player (excellent)
12—9 correct ....novice (good)

Why Kids Can't Write

Too many young Americans can't compose a simple paragraph—or even write well enough to hold a basic job. Here's why—and what you can do to help your children improve this important skill

By ANTHONY BRANDT

These two paragraphs reflect a frightening fact: 15 percent of America's young people are "functionally illiterate," which

(13-year-old)

> I disagree with the Dance from 7 to 9 beacase when your at a dance time goes by so fast and seems like your only there for a little wile only when your having fun and when you go to danses you usually have fun.

> This happen yesterday, their we five kid on a boat. they were all having alot of fun and if you were there you probaly you play with them. Like they were jumping up and down and make believe they were sailing it upside down. They were like jumping off and on. It was very great to be so small and do the same thing there did.

(17-year-old)

means they cannot read—or write—well enough to function at a minimal level in society.

We've all already heard, over and over, that Johnny can't read; yet of the three R's, it is *writing* that gets the least attention in schools, and the writing of American children shows it. Many cannot spell, cannot punctuate a sentence, cannot write coherent, understandable prose.

Clifton Fadiman and James Howard of the Council for Basic Education state the case bluntly: "Our trouble is not that we are not developing good writers. It is that we are not educating people so they can write well enough to keep a job."

Businessmen constantly complain that young job seekers cannot even fill out an application form. College educators feel the problems especially acutely. Says one exasperated ex-English teacher: "It is bad enough that entering students lack a basic knowledge of grammar and punctuation. The *really* sad thing is that very few of them can write a coherent paragraph. Many of the kids *want* to write well and are willing to work at it, but college is not the place to *begin* this task. Writing is a skill that takes years of practice."

Why aren't kids getting this practice? According to Arn and Charlene Tibbetts, authors of *What's Happening to American English?*, much of the decline in writing skills can be attributed to what teachers and administrators call the "Bad Period," a time in the late '60s and early '70s when many high schools abandoned required classes in traditional English language and literature. Instead, students were offered a variety of courses in such subjects as "Sports Literature" and "Mystery Literature." Though fun for the students, few of these courses demanded any writing.

The Bad Period was not an isolated phenomenon, but the end result of a general liberalizing movement in the schools which had been gaining strength since the mid-1960s. Students rebelling against traditional academic pursuits demanded that their courses be "relevant" to their immediate interests. Harassed teachers and administrators responded with "innovative" programs that in effect simply gave the students what they wanted. In the teaching of writing—when it was taught at all—the crucial goals of clarity and coherence were too often replaced by "creativity" and "self-expression."

The Bad Period came to an end in the mid-1970s, but its effects linger. Other factors, too, have kept the situation from improving. Evans Alloway, of the Educational Testing Service in Princeton, N.J., feels that one of today's major problems in the teaching of writing is the large teacher load. The typical English teacher is assigned five classes a day, with about 30 students to a class, for a total of 150 students. If he assigns one theme a week, he must read and correct 150 themes. Assuming he devotes at least ten minutes to each theme, he will add about 25 hours to his workweek. Few teachers are willing or able to take on such a task.

Another factor is the trend toward machine-scored testing, fill-in-the-blank workbooks, and other ways of reducing the amount of time required of teachers and students. The authors of a College Entrance Examination Board report say that "increasing reliance in colleges and high schools on tests requiring only the putting of X's in boxes contributes to juvenile writing delinquency." Yet, ironically, the Scholastic Aptitude Test given by the College Board is itself machine-scored.

How to Improve Your Child's Writing

1. *Dictation*. Before your child learns to write, jot down some of the stories, dreams or adventures he tells you. Then pin your account where he can see it and explain what it is. He'll be delighted by this visible sign of his own speech.

2. *Writing on the wall*. Children love to draw and write on walls. Use this impulse to encourage creativity. Put up a blackboard, or tape brown wrapping paper to the wall. Let them scribble on it.

3. *Notes*. Get your child into the habit of writing notes—"I'm going to Jimmy's house. We're going to play baseball." Keep paper and pencils handy.

4. *Captions*. Buy your child an album, give him pictures to paste into it and let him write captions.

5. *Letters*. A child won't receive mail unless he sends it. Encourage him to write letters to his relatives and friends. Or suggest a pen pal.

6. *Journals*. Encourage your child to keep a journal by giving him a diary. Or help him make his own calendar, leaving plenty of blank space to write down each day's events.

7. *Stories*. Give your child a blank book and let him write short stories, vignettes, or keep a family history.

8. *Shows*. Children rarely realize that television shows and movies start out as pieces of writing. If they don't know what a script looks like, borrow one from the library. Encourage them to write their own.

9. *The "feely" game*. Build a "feely" box (a large box with a hole just big enough for a hand to get through) and put different objects in it. Then have the child feel the objects and write descriptions of them.

10. *Directions*. The next time you need to write directions, have one of your older children do it instead. Make sure he's precise: "Turn onto Green Street." Yes, but which way? Ask the child to think through the whole trip and put it into words.

Whatever the reason, students are being required to do less writing, and are therefore less and less able to write. To compound the problem, teachers very often cannot write well themselves and have had no training in the teaching of writing. According to Donald Graves, head of the Writing Process Lab at the University of New Hampshire, a recent survey showed that among 222 education courses for future teachers offered at 36 universities, only two were in the teaching of writing.

But the problem is not solely the fault of our educational system. Schools reflect trends in society, and there is plenty of evidence that Americans in general are doing less writing. Instead of writing a letter, we pick up the phone. Television is another major culprit. A Surgeon General's report has concluded that some children who watch television are easily distracted, more passive and generally less creative. And obviously, if they are watching TV, they are not writing.

Yet the need for good writing is as critical as it ever was. Newspapers, magazines, books and professional journals; movie and TV scripts; job descriptions, advertisements, business letters and police reports; financial forms, questionnaires; instructions for using products; medical records; journals, diaries and personal letters; catalogues—all these things and many more are *written*. And if they aren't written well, some of us—sometimes all of us—will suffer.

Beyond practical considerations lie considerations of personal improvement. The impulse to communicate something of ourselves is universal; it's part of being human. In poetry, in the stories we write, in our diaries and journals, in letters to friends and family, we give form to thoughts and to feelings—in effect, to ourselves. An inability to communicate in this way can be a major disadvantage.

The decline in writing skills *can* be stopped. Today's back-to-basics movement has already forced some schools to place renewed emphasis on the three R's, and the teaching of writing is becoming a hot topic among educators. Although the inability of some teachers to teach writing successfully remains a big stumbling block, a number of programs have been developed to attack this problem. Perhaps the best known is the Bay Area Writing Project, founded by James Gray in 1974. Every summer, 25 to 30 English teachers spend five weeks at the Berkeley campus of the University of California, where they are taught to teach writing. When these teachers return to their schools, they conduct training programs of their own. The idea has spread throughout the country, and Gray now administers a National Writing Project with 80 sites from coast to coast.

But widespread change for the better will come only with strong parental involvement. Some of the questions parents ought to ask are: How much writing is my child required to do in school? (If the average is fewer than three pages a week, your child is not writing enough.) Is his writing evaluated for clarity, coherence and readability, as well as for mechanical errors? Do teachers of all my child's courses require writing?

(There's no reason why writing should be confined to the English department.)

Remember: The schools belong to you; your tax money pays all those salaries. If writing is poorly taught in your school, *demand* improvement from all concerned.

(13-year-old)

I disagree with the Dance from 7 to 9 beacase when your at a dance time goes by so fast and seems like your only there for a little wile only when your having fun and when you go to danses you usually have fun.

(17-year-old)

This happen yesterday, their we five kid on a boat. They were all having alot of fun and if you were there you probaly you play with them. Like they were jumping up and down and make believe they were sailing it upside down. They were like jumping off and on. It was very great to be so small and do the same thing there did.

Word Power Test No. 10

Of Knights, Castles and Fair Ladies

By PETER FUNK

The Age of Chivalry is not dead. Many of its most evocative words live on in modern English. All of the test words below, for example, have come down to us from the days of knights, castles, tournaments and fair ladies. Pick what you believe to be the correct answer and check your results after this test.

1. **investiture** (in vĕs′ tĭ cher)—having to do with A: trust. B: money. C: ceremony. D: denial.
2. **sanctuary** (sank′ chōō ĕr ē)—A: statue. B: market. C: ruin. D: place of refuge.
3. **accouterments** (a kōō′ ter ments)—A: romantic songs. B: accessories. C: compliments. D: compromises.
4. **ordnance**—A: basic system. B: military equipment. C: authoritative decree. D: state treasury.
5. **citadel** (cit′ ă d'l)—A: mountain. B: conduit. C: palace. D: fortress.
6. **rampart** (ram′ part)—A: tall tower. B: heavy gate. C: bridge. D: bulwark.

7. **esquire** (es′ kwīr)—A: knight's attendant. B: nobleman. C: palace guard. D: administrator.

8. **churlish**—A: brave. B: foolish. C: boorish. D: shy.

9. **alms** (ahmz)—A: charity. B: gratuity. C: prayer. D: stipend.

10. **pavilion** (pă vĭl′ yun)—A: balcony. B: terrace. C: tent. D: walled garden.

11. **joust** (jowst)—A: oath. B: personal combat. C: heavy beam. D: jest.

12. **pagan** (pā′ gan)—A: joyful song. B: bigot. C: foreigner. D: unbeliever.

13. **accolade** (ăk′ ō lād)—A: courtesy. B: affront. C: honor. D: awareness.

14. **dub**—A: to replace. B: name. C: bungle. D: restrain.

15. **quest**—A: search. B: foolishness. C: spirituality. D: purity.

16. **lackey**—A: flunky. B: beggar. C: dullard. D: buffoon.

17. **crenelate** (krĕn′ uh lāt)—A: to notch. B: ruffle. C: taper. D: dress.

18. **vigil** (vĭj′ ĭl)—A: long journey. B: young nun. C: celebration. D: watchful wakefulness.

19. **gauntlet** (gŏnt′ lĭt)—A: sleeve. B: defiance. C: glove. D: small hawk.

20. **paladin** (pal′ uh din)—A: gatehouse. B: legendary champion. C: felon. D: armored horse.

ANSWERS

1. **investiture**—C: The ceremony of clothing with the robes of office; a formal installation; as, the *investiture* of an Eagle Scout. Latin.

2. **sanctuary**—D: Place of refuge. From Latin *sanctus* (holy); therefore a place such as a church. where, traditionally, a fugitive could find safety and shelter.

3. **accouterments**—B: Accessories such as clothing or furnishings; as, the *accouterments* of battle. Old French *acoustrer*.

4. **ordnance**—B: Military equipment, including weapons, ammunition, supplies and vehicles. Old French *ordenance* (arrangement).

5. **citadel**—D: Fortress dominating a city; stronghold. Italian *cittadella* (little city).

6. **rampart**—D: Bulwark; an earth embankment that fortifies;

anything that protects; as, the *ramparts* of freedom. Provençal *amparar*.

7. **esquire**—A: Young man attending a knight. Later, any gentleman, but today used primarily by lawyers. Old French *esquier* (shield bearer).

8. **churlish**—C: Boorish; surly; vulgar: intentionally rude; as, *churlish* manners. Old English *ceorl* (peasant, man of low rank).

9. **alms**—A: Charity; as, to give *alms* to the beggar. Old English *aelmysse*.

10. **pavilion**—C: Large, ornate, peaked tent. Old French *paveillun* (tent) from Latin *papilio* (butterfly). Also, a section of a building.

11. **joust**—B: Personal combat, especially between mounted knights; any one-on-one competition. Old French *juste*.

12. **pagan**—D: Unbeliever. When the Roman Empire was Christianized, folk living in a *pagus* (Latin for village) were suspected of idolatry.

13. **accolade**—C: Honor; recognition; specifically, the ceremony of conferring knighthood. Provençal *acolada* (embrace). "The performance received universal *accolades*."

14. **dub**—B: To name; nickname; characterize; as, to *dub* the giant "Little John." Originally, to touch with a sword, bestowing knighthood. Old Frisian *aduber* (to invest with dignity).

15. **quest**—A: Search; an adventurous expedition by a knight. Old French *queste* (official inquiry).

16. **lackey**—A: Flunky; bootlicker; one who does menial chores. Old French *laquais* (footman).

17. **crenelate**—A: To make squared notches in the battlement of a fortress. From Vulgar Latin *crena* (a notch).

18. **vigil**—D: A watchful wakefulness; as, a mother's *vigil* beside a sick child. Also, the eve of a religious festival. Latin *vigilare* (to watch).

19. **gauntlet**—C: Leather glove. To "take up the gauntlet" is to accept a challenge. Old French *gant* (glove).

20. **paladin**—B: Legendary champion; outstanding person; defender of a noble cause; as, Sir Ernest Shackleton, the *paladin* of explorers. Originally, one of Charlemagne's twelve peers. Old French *palasm* (belonging to the palace).

VOCABULARY RATINGS

20—18 correct ....master (exceptional)
17—13 correct .... player (excellent)
12—9 correct ....novice (good)

The Stranger
Who Taught Magic

By ARTHUR GORDON

That July morning, I remember, was like any other, calm and
opalescent before the heat of the fierce Georgia sun. I was 13:
sunburned, shaggy-haired, a little aloof, and solitary. In winter
I had to put on shoes and go to school like everyone else. But
summers I lived by the sea, and my mind was empty and wild
and free.

On this particular morning, I had tied my rowboat to the
pilings of an old dock upriver from our village. There, sometimes, the striped sheepshead lurked in the still, green water.
I was crouched, motionless as a stone, when a voice spoke
suddenly above my head: "Canst thou draw out leviathan with
a hook, or his tongue with a cord which thou lettest down?"

I looked up, startled, into a lean, pale face and a pair of the
most remarkable eyes I had ever seen. It wasn't a question of
color; I'm not sure, now, what color they were. It was a combination of things: warmth, humor, interest, alertness. Intensity—that's the word, I guess—and, underlying it all, a curious kind of mocking sadness. I believe I thought him old.

He saw how taken aback I was. "Sorry," he said. "It's a bit early in the morning for the Book of Job, isn't it?" He nodded at the two or three fish in the boat. "Think you could teach me how to catch those?"

Ordinarily, I was wary of strangers, but anyone interested in fishing was hardly a stranger. I nodded, and he climbed down into the boat. "Perhaps we should introduce ourselves," he said. "But then again, perhaps not. You're a boy willing to teach, I'm a teacher willing to learn. That's introduction enough. I'll call you 'Boy,' and you call me 'Sir.'"

Such talk sounded strange in my world of sun and salt water. But there was something so magnetic about the man, and so disarming about his smile, that I didn't care.

I handed him a hand line and showed him how to bait his hooks with fiddler crabs. He kept losing baits, because he could not recognize a sheepshead's stealthy tug, but he seemed content not to catch anything. He told me he had rented one of the weathered bungalows behind the dock. "I needed to hide for a while," he said. "Not from the police, or anything like that. Just from friends and relatives. So don't tell anyone you've found me, will you?"

I was tempted to ask where he was from; there was a crispness in the way he spoke that was very different from the soft accents I was accustomed to. But I didn't. He had said he was a teacher, though, and so I asked what he taught.

"In the school catalogue they call it English," he said. "But I like to think of it as a course in magic—in the mystery and magic of words. Are you fond of words?"

I said that I had never thought much about them. I also pointed out that the tide was ebbing, that the current was too strong for more fishing, and that in any case it was time for breakfast.

"Of course," he said, pulling in his line. "I'm a little forgetful about such things these days." He eased himself back onto the dock with a little grimace, as if the effort cost him something. "Will you be back on the river later?"

I said that I would probably go casting for shrimp at low tide.

"Stop by," he said. "We'll talk about words for a while, and then perhaps you can show me how to catch shrimp."

So began a most unlikely friendship, because I did go back.
To this day, I'm not sure why. Perhaps it was because, for the
first time, I had met an adult on terms that were in balance.
In the realm of words and ideas, he might be the teacher. But
in my own small universe of winds and tides and sea creatures,
the wisdom belonged to me.

Almost every day after that, we'd go wherever the sea gods
or my whim decreed. Sometimes up the silver creeks, where
the terrapin skittered down the banks and the great blue herons
stood like statues. Sometimes along the ocean dunes, fringed
with graceful sea oats, where by night the great sea turtles
crawled and by day the wild goats browsed. I showed him
where the mullet swirled and where the flounder lay in cunning
camouflage. I learned that he was incapable of much exertion;
even pulling up the anchor seemed to exhaust him. But he
never complained. And, all the time, talk flowed from him like
a river.

Much of it I have forgotten now, but some comes back as
clear and distinct as if it all happened yesterday, not decades
ago. We might be sitting on a hollow of the dunes, watching
the sun go down in a smear of crimson. "Words," he'd say.
"Just little black marks on paper. Just sounds in the empty air.
But think of the power they have! They can make you laugh
or cry, love or hate, fight or run away. They can heal or hurt.
They even come to look and sound like what they mean. Angry
looks angry on the page. Ugly *sounds* ugly when you say it.
Here!" He would hand me a piece of shell. "Write a word that
looks or sounds like what it means."

I would stare helplessly at the sand.

"Oh," he'd cry, "you're being dense. There are so many!
Like whisper . . . leaden . . . twilight . . . chime. Tell you what:
when you go to bed tonight, think of five words that look like
what they mean and five that sound like what they mean. Don't
go to sleep until you do!"

And I would try—but always fall asleep.

Or we might be anchored just offshore, casting into the surf
for sea bass, our little bateau nosing over the rollers like a
restless hound. "Rhythm," he would say. "Life is full of it;
words should have it, too. But you have to train your ear.
Listen to the waves on a quiet night; you'll pick up the cadence.

Look at the patterns the wind makes in dry sand and you'll see how syllables in a sentence should fall. Do you know what I mean?"

My conscious self didn't know; but perhaps something deep inside me did. In any case, I listened.

I listened, too, when he read from the books he sometimes brought: Kipling, Conan Doyle, Tennyson's *Idylls of the King*. Often he would stop and repeat a phrase or a line that pleased him. One day, in Malory's *Le Morte d'Arthur,* he found one: "And the great horse grimly neighed." "Close your eyes," he said to me, "and say that slowly, out loud." I did. "How did it make you feel?" "It gives me the shivers," I said truthfully. He was delighted.

But the magic that he taught was not confined to words; he had a way of generating in me an excitement about things I had always taken for granted. He might point to a bank of clouds. "What do you see there? Colors? That's not enough. Look for towers and drawbridges. Look for dragons and griffins and strange and wonderful beasts."

Or he might pick up an angry, claw-brandishing blue crab, holding it cautiously by the back flippers as I had taught him. "Pretend you're this crab," he'd say. "What do you see through those stalk-like eyes? What do you feel with those complicated legs? What goes on in your tiny brain? Try it for just five seconds. Stop being a boy. Be a crab!" And I would stare in amazement at the furious creature, feeling my comfortable identity lurch and sway under the impact of the idea.

So the days went by. Our excursions became less frequent, because he tired so easily. He brought two chairs down to the dock and some books, but he didn't read much. He seemed content to watch me as I fished, or the circling gulls, or the slow river coiling past.

A sudden shadow fell across my life when my parents told me I was going to camp for two weeks. On the dock that afternoon I asked my friend if he would be there when I got back. "I hope so," he said gently.

But he wasn't. I remember standing on the sun-warmed planking of the old dock, staring at the shuttered bungalow and feeling a hollow sense of finality and loss. I ran to Jackson's grocery store—where everyone knew everything—and asked where the schoolteacher had gone.

"He was sick, real sick," Mrs. Jackson replied. "Doc phoned his relatives up north to come get him. He left something for you—he figured you'd be asking after him."

She handed me a book. It was a slender volume of verse, *Flame and Shadow,* by someone I had never heard of: Sara Teasdale. The corner of one page was turned down, and there was a penciled star by one of the poems. I still have the book, with that poem, "On the Dunes."

> If there is any life when death is over,
> These tawny beaches will know much of me,
> I shall come back, as constant and as changeful
> : As the unchanging, many-colored sea.
> If life was small, if it has made me scornful,
> Forgive me; I shall straighten like a flame
> In the great calm of death, and if you want me
> Stand on the sea-ward dunes and call my name.

Well, I have never stood on the dunes and called his name. For one thing, I never knew it; for another, I'd be too self-conscious. And there are long stretches when I forget all about him. But sometimes—when the music or the magic in a phrase makes my skin tingle, or when I pick up an angry blue crab, or when I see a dragon in the flaming sky—sometimes I remember.

Word Power Test No. 11

Words to Tax Your Brain and Bank Account

By PETER FUNK

It's hard to remember these days that our country was founded partly to avoid taxation. Taxes are also hard to escape in our everyday language: in fact, all the following words are relatives of that ubiquitous word. "Tax," appropriately, comes from the Latin *tangere* (to touch) and its offspring *taxare* (to touch or appraise). And each test word also has *tangere* as an ancestor. Check the word or phrase you believe is *nearest in meaning* to the key word. Answers appear after this test.

1. **tact** (tăkt)—A: implication, B: graceful sensitivity. C: relevance. D: direction of a sailing boat.
2. **attain** (a tāne')—A: to achieve. B: approach. C: enclose. D: select.
3. **entirety** (en tīr' tē)—A: completeness. B: entailment. C: infinity. D: duration.
4. **tainted** (tān' tid)—A: dyed. B: unresponsive. C: blamed. D: contaminated.

5. **contingency** (kon tin' jen sē)—A: expectation. B: improvisation. C: possible occurrence. D: continuation.
6. **tactile** (tăk' t'l)—Pertaining to: A: sense of touch. B: strategy. C: firmness. D: stickiness.
7. **integrity** (in tĕg' rĭ tē)—A: good judgment. B: benevolence. C: honesty. D: fearlessness.
8. **surtax** (sur' tăks)—A: tax relief. B: penalty. C: extra tax. D: partial payment.
9. **contiguous** (kon tĭg' yew us)—A: proximate. B: distant. C: emergent. D: disparate.
10. **tasteful** (tāst' full)—A: winsome. B: fulsome. C: zesty. D: attractive.
11. **propitiate** (pro pish i āt)—A: to evict. B: assist. C: praise. D: appease.
12. **integer** (in' tĕ jer)—A: differentiation. B: a whole. C: rectitude. D: period of time between events.
13. **tango** (tang' go)—A: tropic fruit. B: outburst. C: desperate situation. D: a dance.
14. **integral** (in' tĕ gr'l)—A: essential. B: in combination with. C: complicated. D: simple.
15. **tax** (tăks)—A: to harass. B: burden. C: penalize. D: treat unfairly.
16. **integrate** (in' tĕ grāt)—A: to question. B: involve. C: systematize. D: unify.
17. **intangible** (in tan' jĭ b'l)—A: nonexistent. B: having a religious meaning. C: irregular. D: without physical substance.
18. **contagion** (kon tāy' jun)—A: concealment. B: an infecting contact. C: worrisome question. D: lack of concern.
19. **intact** (in tăkt')—A: removed. B: entire. C: permanent. D: innermost.
20. **taskmaster** (task' master)—A: rigorous supervisor. B: surrogate. C: pacesetter. D: dictator.

ANSWERS

1. **tact**—B: Graceful sensitivity in doing or saying the right thing. "Arguing with a tax auditor requires *tact*." Latin *tactus* (sense of touch).
2. **attain**—A: Achieve; accomplish. "He hopes to *attain* his

goal—a college degree—by passing the required courses."
Latin *ad* (to) and *tangere*.

3. **entirety**—A: Completeness; sum total. "The IRS ordered a review of the tax return in its *entirety*." Through Old French *entiereté* from Latin *integritas* (unimpaired condition), from *integer* (whole).

4. **tainted**—D: Contaminated. *Tainted* meat is touched with incipient decay. A *tainted* reputation is caused by reports of misconduct. A blend, ultimately, from Latin *ad* (to) plus *tangere* and *tingere* (to stain).

5. **contingency**—C: A possible unforeseen occurrence; emergency; accident; as, a reserve fund to cover any *contingency*. Latin *contingens* (touching on all sides).

6. **tactile**—A: Pertaining to a sense of touch; tangible; as, *tactile* communication between monkeys. Latin *tactus*.

7. **integrity**—C: Uncompromising honesty; firm adherence to a code of values; soundness; as, the *integrity* of our judicial system. Latin *integritas*.

8. **surtax**—C: An extra or additional tax; as, a proposal for a five-percent *surtax* on family incomes over $15,000. Latin *sur* (above) and *taxare*.

9. **contiguous**—A: Proximate; in actual touch or almost touching. "Portugal is *contiguous* to Spain." Latin *contingens*.

10. **tasteful**—D: Attractive; done according to good taste. "The room's decor is *tasteful*." Vulgar Latin *tastare* from *taxare*.

11. **propitiate**—D: To appease; cause to be favorably disposed; conciliate; as, to *propitiate* the gods. Latin *propitiare* to (soothe).

12. **integer**—B: A whole; entity; anything complete in itself. "The nation was unified, as *integer* of like-minded people." Latin *integer*.

13. **tango**—D: A Latin American dance with long gliding steps and dips. Through Spanish *tangir* (to play an instrument) from Latin *tangere*.

14. **integral**—A: Essential to completeness; indispensable. "The heart is an *integral* part of the body." Latin *integer*.

15. **tax**—B: To put a heavy burden on, or to place under a heavy strain; wear out. "An excessive delay may *tax* one's patience." Latin *taxare*.

16. **integrate**—D: To unify; blend various parts together into a whole. A conglomerate tries to *integrate* several companies into its organization. Also, to abolish racial segregation. Latin *integrare* (to make whole).

17. **intangible**—D: Without physical substance and therefore incapable of being seen, touched, etc.; imperceptible. "Goodwill in business is an *intangible* asset." Latin *intangibilis*.

18. **contagion**—B: An infecting contact, good or bad; the spreading of a disease, influence, attitude, doctrine. "A *contagion* of hope swept the country." Latin *contagio* (a touching).

19. **intact**—B: Entire; complete and unimpaired; having no parts missing. "Congress emerged from the crisis with its function and authority *intact*." Latin *intactus* (untouched).

20. **taskmaster**—A: Rigorous supervisor; someone who assigns difficult work and is exacting or harsh while overseeing its completion. Latin *taxare* and *magister* (master).

VOCABULARY RATINGS

20—18 correct ....master (exceptional)
17—13 correct .... player (excellent)
12—9 correct ....novice (good)

How Will You Know Unless I Tell You?

Too often we forget how much a spontaneous word of appreciation can mean

By JANE LINDSTROM

Cold spring rain slashed across the window, further lowering my spirits, already depressed by long convalescence from surgery. Get-well cards had stopped coming. A faded chrysanthemum plant, a gift from fellow teachers, was all that remained of the flowers I had received. I felt lonely, unimportant, forgotten by a world that apparently was doing very well without me.

Then the mail arrived, bringing a note from a casual acquaintance, a teacher I passed each morning on my way to school. "Dear Jane," she said. "My class is about to begin, but I must write these few words before my students arrive. I missed your smile and your wave this morning, just as I have every day since you've been ill. I pray you'll be well soon. You're probably surprised at receiving this note, but the world for me is a less happy place without you. And how will you know unless I tell you?"

Suddenly, the paralyzing sense of despair slipped away. Someone missed me; someone needed me. That knowledge proved more effective than any medicine the doctor could pre-scribe.

I reread the words carefully, savoring each one. The last sentence held my attention: "How will you know unless I tell you?" I wouldn't have known, of course, and I would still have been lonely and depressed. How can any of us know what's in the minds and hearts of others—unless we receive some word, some gesture?

Most of us in this sophisticated, dehumanized age tend to place check-reins on our emotions. We withhold words of love, admiration and approval. And yet those words might give some unhappy person a moment of joy or help him cope with deep despair. They might even become the few bright threads in the dull fabric of his life.

I recalled that on my last visit to the supermarket the man ahead of me smiled warmly at the harried checkout girl and complimented her for bagging his purchases so carefully. She seemed startled at this unexpected praise, but her face lighted up, and the tired, tense lines disappeared. She thanked him warmly, then turned to wait on me with a bright smile and cheerful word. Chances are that the hundreds of people she served that day caught the glow and passed it on to others.

Everyone, if he is to do his best, needs to be noticed and appreciated. Each of us has countless opportunities at work, at school, on the subway or bus, to speak out and meet those needs. And in doing so we may set off chain reactions of goodwill.

Of course, we can't always play Pollyanna. There are times when adverse criticism is justified. And how it is given can make all the difference. I know a woman who speaks out when she is dissatisfied, but prefaces her complaints with recognition of some worthwhile achievement. If it's appropriate and she can do so tactfully, she offers suggestions for improvement. She has discovered that her criticisms are usually welcomed and that her suggestions are accepted courteously.

She's discovered, too, that as a rule people labor to please others rather than themselves. Most of us want to be told how we are doing. If our best efforts are met with silence, we tend to become careless and negligent.

We face choices every day. We can speak out or say nothing. Our decision may not affect anyone. But then again it may.

It may even, on rare occasions, determine the course of a human life.

A young student teacher I once knew was assigned to instruct sixth-graders for one week at a school outdoor center. She enthusiastically and painstakingly planned a variety of experiences for these city youngsters, hoping to share with them her love of the fields and woods. But the week was a complete disaster. It rained four of the five days, and the children were rowdy and uncoöperative. When at last the youngsters were packing to return to town, the student teacher came to me in tears. "I wasn't sure before," she said, "but now I know. I can never work with children. I'm just not cut out for it."

What a loss! With just a little more maturity and experience, this fine, sensitive young woman would make an outstanding teacher. But I knew I couldn't change her mind.

Then, as the children scrambled aboard the bus, one girl lingered behind and, after a moment, said to the student teacher, "I want to thank you for this week and for the things you taught us. You know, I never listened to the wind in the trees before. It's a lovely sound, and I'll never forget it. Here's a poem I wrote for you. I almost didn't give it to you." She pulled a slip of paper from her pocket, then ran to join the others.

After reading the few penciled lines, the young teacher looked up with tears in her eyes, but now they were tears of happiness. I breathed a prayer of thanks to this one child who had made the right choice. I knew that because of her gesture countless children would enjoy the affection and guidance of a fine teacher.

If words of loving approval are so important at the beginning of a career, they are even more important at the beginning of life. Children have not yet learned from experience that time heals most sorrows, that bad times are followed by good, that failures are usually interspersed with successes. Admittedly, they must have guidance and consistent discipline if they are to become sound citizens. But above all else, children crave spoken assurances of love and approval. Love locked in our hearts doesn't reach them; it is like a letter written and not sent. If they are to become emotionally secure, they must hear: I love you. I'm proud of you. I'm glad you're here. A soft voice, friendly eyes and gentle words will convey the message even to a baby.

People of all ages and backgrounds, at all stages of success or failure, need love and recognition in order to live happily. We need them in order to defeat those two arch-enemies of human happiness—loneliness and insignificance.

None of us wants to be a fraud, to flatter, or put into words emotions we don't feel. Such insincerity is easily spotted, and it benefits no one—it is, in fact, a form of cheating. But isn't it cheating, too, when we withhold words that someone may desperately need to hear?

The note that had started this train of thought was still in my hand, and an idea was not long in coming. I had a long-overdue message to deliver—and would deliver it in person as soon as I could. Several miles from my home, an elderly farmwife had cleared the roadside of litter and planted flowers in its place. I never passed by without a feeling of joy, a lifting of the spirit that lingered through the day. Surely the farmwife would be happy to know that. But how would she know unless I told her?

Word Power Test No. 12

A Poet Doffs Her Hat

By PETER FUNK

Emily Dickinson (1830–1886), one of America's most perceptive and popular poets, once wrote: "I don't know of anything so mighty as words. There are those to which I lift my hat when I see them sitting princelike on the page." The following "hat-lifting" words are from her poems. Pick the definition you think is correct. Check your results at the end of this test.

1. **reverie** (rev′ er ē)—A: daydream. B: adoration. C: awakening call. D: meeting.
2. **inebriate** (in ē′ brē it)—one who is A: a beginner. B: intoxicated. C: a specialist. D: puffed up.
3. **ecstatic**—A: clairvoyant. B: bewildered. C: spellbound. D: fitful.
4. **genteel** (jen tēl′)—A: shy. B: well-bred. C: supercilious. D: smiling.
5. **obviate** (ob′ vē āt)—A: to point out. B: make unnecessary. C: clarify. D: improve.

6. **bog**—A: covered hole. B: sandbar. C: narrow valley. D: small marsh.

7. **nonchalant** (non shuh lahnt')—A: calm and casual. B: listless. C: apprehensive. D: negligent.

8. **amethyst** (am' uh thist)—A: blue. B: yellow. C: purple or violet. D: puce.

9. **dissembling**—A: weakening. B: pretending. C: taking apart. D: scattering.

10. **prosaic** (prō zā' ik)—A: wordy. B: terse. C: efficient. D: unimaginative.

11. **comely** (kum' lē)—A: harmonious. B: peaceful. C: friendly. D: attractive.

12. **phlegmatic** (fleg mat' ik)—A: sick. B: ignorant. C: sluggish. D: bloated.

13. **palpitate**—A: to flutter or beat rapidly. B: be aware of by touching. C: grow soft. D: twist back and forth.

14. **inference**—A: reasoned deduction. B: secret. C: reservation. D: idea.

15. **interdict** (in' ter dict)—A: accusation of wrongdoing. B: whatever is temporary. C: decree forbidding something. D: appeal.

16. **precarious** (pre kair' ē us)—A: harsh. B: wary. C: ill. D: risky.

17. **illusion** (il lu' zhun)—A: daze. B: reference. C: diagram. D: deception.

18. **abstemious** (ab stē' mē us)—in the use of food, A: moderate. B: fussy. C: indulgent. D: delicate.

19. **posthumous** (pŏs' choo mus)—A: causing laughter. B: slow in progressing. C: organic. D: happening after death.

20. **unimpeachable**—A: without hope. B: out of danger. C: above suspicion. D: not acceptable.

ANSWERS

1. **reverie**—A: Daydream of pleasant things. French *rêver* (to dream). "To make a prairie it takes a clover and one bee, and *reverie*. The *reverie* alone will do, if bees are few."

2. **inebriate**—B: One who is intoxicated, excited, exhilarated. Latin *inebriare* (to make drunk).

3. **ecstatic**—C: Spellbound or enraptured by intense joy. Greek *existanai* (to derange).

4. **genteel**—B: Well-bred; courteous; free from vulgarity or rudeness; as, a *genteel* manner. Middle French *gentil* (gentle).

5. **obviate**—B: To make unnecessary; do away with difficulties. Latin *obviare* (to prevent).

6. **bog**—D: Small marsh; wet, spongy ground. Gaelic *bogach*. "How public like a frog, to tell one's name the livelong June to an admiring *bog*."

7. **nonchalant**—A: Calm and casual; as, "How *nonchalant* the hedge!" French *nonchaloir* (to be unconcerned).

8. **amethyst**—C: Purple or violet color. Greek *amethystos* (not drunken): the gem was worn to ward off drunkenness. "I'll tell you how the sun rose—a ribbon at a time. The steeples swam in *amethyst*, the news, like squirrels, ran."

9. **dissembling**—B: Pretending; giving a false appearance. Latin *dissimulare* (to be unlike).

10. **prosaic**—D: Unimaginative; having no poetic beauty; dull; as, "a few *prosaic* days." Latin *prosa* (prose).

11. **comely**—D: Attractive; pleasing to the sight; as, a *comely* young couple. Middle English *comly*.

12. **phlegmatic**—C: Sluggish; not easily excited; apathetic; as, "those old *phlegmatic* mountains." Greek *phlegmatikos* (inflamed).

13. **palpitate**—A: To flutter or beat rapidly, as heart action from emotion; pulsate; as, the *palpitating* mirage. Latin *palpare* (to stroke).

14. **inference**—A: Reasoned deduction; loosely, a reasonable guess based on available evidence. Latin *inferre* (to bring in).

15. **interdict**—C: Decree that prohibits someone from doing something. Latin *interdicere* (to forbid).

16. **precarious**—D: Risky; uncertain; as, a *precarious* situation. Latin *precarius* (obtained by begging).

17. **illusion**—D: Deception; false or misleading impression; as, youthful *illusions*. Latin *illudere* (to deceive).

18. **abstemious**—A: Moderate and sparing in food, drink or pleasure; not self-indulgent. Latin *abstemius*.

19. **posthumous**—D: Happening after one's death. Latin *postumus*, from *post* (after) and *humus* (earth).

20. **unimpeachable**—C: Above suspicion; unquestionably true. *Un-* (not) and Latin *impedicare* (to entangle).

VOCABULARY RATINGS

20—18 correct ....master (exceptional)
17—13 correct .... player (excellent)
12—9 correct ....novice (good)

The Open Window

A master wordsmith concocts a classic tale of horror and hilarity

By SAKI

"My aunt will be down presently, Mr. Nuttel," said a self-possessed young lady of 15. "In the meantime you must put up with me."

Framton Nuttel endeavored to say the correct something to flatter the niece without unduly discounting the aunt. Privately he doubted whether these formal visits on total strangers would help the nerve cure which he was supposed to be undergoing in this rural retreat.

"I'll give you letters to everyone I know there," his sister had said. "Or else you'll bury yourself and not speak to a soul, and your nerves will be worse than ever from moping."

"Do you know many people around here?" asked the niece when she judged they had had sufficient silent communion.

"Hardly a soul," said Framton. "My sister visited here four years ago, and she gave me letters of introduction."

"Then you know practically nothing about my aunt?" pursued the young lady.

"Only her name and address."

"Her great tragedy happened just three years ago," said the child. "That would be since your sister's time."

"Her tragedy?" asked Framton. Somehow in this restful spot tragedies seemed out of place.

"You may wonder why we keep that window open so late in the year," said the niece, indicating a large french window that opened on to a lawn. "Out through that window, three years ago to a day, her husband and her two young brothers went off for their day's shooting. In crossing the moor they were engulfed in a treacherous bog. Their bodies were never recovered."

Here the child's voice faltered. "Poor Aunt always thinks that they'll come back someday, they and the little brown spaniel that was lost with them, and walk in at the window. That is why it is kept open every evening till dusk. She has often told me how they went out, her husband with his white waterproof coat over his arm. You know, sometimes on still evenings like this, I get a creepy feeling that they *will* all walk in through that window..."

She broke off with a little shudder. It was a relief to Framton when the aunt bustled into the room with a whirl of apologies for being late.

"I hope you don't mind the open window," she said. "My husband and brothers will be home from shooting, and they always come in this way."

She rattled on cheerfully about the prospects for duck in the winter. Framton made a desperate effort to turn the talk on to a less ghastly topic, conscious that his hostess was giving him only a fragment of her attention, and that her eyes were constantly straying past him to the open window.

"The doctors order me a complete rest from mental excitement and physical exercise," announced Framton, who labored under the widespread delusion that total strangers are hungry for the last detail of one's infirmities.

"Oh?" responded Mrs. Sappleton, vaguely. Then she suddenly brightened into alert attention—but not to what Framton was saying.

"Here they are at last!" she cried. "In time for tea."

Framton shivered slightly and turned toward the niece with a look of sympathetic comprehension. The child was staring through the open window with dazed horror in her eyes. Framton swung round and looked in the same direction.

In the deepening twilight three figures were walking noiselessly across the lawn, a tired brown spaniel close at their heels. They all carried guns, and one had a white coat over his shoulders.

Framton grabbed his walking stick; the hall door and the gravel drive were dimly noted stages in his headlong retreat.

"Here we are, my dear," said the bearer of the white mackintosh, coming in through the window. "Who was that who bolted out as we came up?"

"A Mr. Nuttel," said Mrs. Sappleton, "who dashed off without a word of apology when you arrived. One would think he had seen a ghost."

"I expect it was the spaniel," said the niece calmly. "He told me he had a horror of dogs. He was once hunted into a cemetery on the banks of the Ganges by a pack of pariah dogs, and had to spend the night in a newly dug grave with the creatures snarling and foaming above him. Enough to make anyone lose their nerve."

Romance at short notice was her specialty.

IT PAYS TO ENRICH YOUR WORD POWER ®

Word Power Test No. 13

Short and Snappy Words

By PETER FUNK

Short words aren't necessarily simple words. But they have a kind of terse muscularity that endows a spoken or written statement with power and vigor. Check the word or phrase that you believe is *nearest in meaning* to the key word. Answers appear after this test.

1. **awe**—A: wonder and fear. B: extreme bewilderment. C: shyness. D: surprise.
2. **flinch**—A: to grimace. B: recoil. C: squint. D: tighten or stiffen.
3. **sere**—A: dried up. B: wise. C: charred. D: thin.
4. **horde**—A: a gathering. B: hidden supplies. C: sparseness. D: large crowd.
5. **pact**—A: offer. B: cargo. C: agreement. D: evasion.
6. **ebb**—A: ripple. B: decline. C: dispersion. D: advance.
7. **caste**—A: mold. B: exclusive class. C: troupe. D: angling tactic.
8. **norm**—A: a constant. B: survey. C: standard. D: parasite.

9. **knoll**—A: a fairy-tale monster. B: ornament. C: clamor. D: hillock.

10. **hew**—A: to obey. B: chop. C: cry out. D: tinge.

11. **churn**—A: to stir vigorously. B: twist and turn. C: go in circles. D: vacillate.

12. **daft**—A: breezy. B: awkward. C: silly. D: nimble.

13. **shard**—A: agricultural tool. B: blunt instrument. C: covering. D: residue.

14. **bleak**—A: plain and simple. B: dreary. C: festive. D: feeble.

15. **laud**—A: to decry. B: praise. C: encourage. D: criticize.

16. **spawn**—A: to respond. B: stimulate. C: reject. D: produce.

17. **cult**—A: snobbery. B: tastefulness. C: sect. D: yearling.

18. **brunt**—A: full impact. B: abrupt manner. C: surfeit. D: rumor.

19. **scope**—A: epoch. B: range of thoughts. C: surmise. D: agenda.

20. **brash**—A: impetuous. B: boastful. C: sarcastic. D: noisy.

ANSWERS

1. **awe**—A: Profound wonder tinged with fear; as, "the decline in *awe* of American strength." Middle English *aghe* from Old Norse *agi* (awe, fear).

2. **flinch**—B: To recoil or shrink from; wince. "Most wives might *flinch* at such baffling monologues." Old French *flenchir* (to turn aside).

3. **sere**—A: Dried up; withered; as, "the Yucatan Peninsula's *sere* plain." Old English *sear* (dry).

4. **horde**—D: A large crowd; mass; throng; as, "*hordes* of passengers." Turkish *ordu* (camp, army).

5. **pact**—C: Agreement between persons; covenant. "Before they cried themselves to sleep that night, they made a *pact*." The Latin *paciscere* (to agree) is related to *pax* (peace).

6. **ebb**—B: Decline; fading away. "It marked the lowest *ebb* in their dealings with Ann." The literal meaning is the return of tidewater to the sea. Old English *ebbian* (low tide).

7. **caste**—B: Exclusive class, especially in India; as, "a *caste* system, with men as the executives and women as the clerical workers." The Portuguese *casta* (race, breed) was adapted by India in the 16th century.

8. **norm**—C: A standard; a model serving as a guide; as, "a breakdown in common *norms* of etiquette." Latin *norma* (carpenter's square).

9. **knoll**—D: A hillock; mound. "Here on a *knoll* was the clump of thorn apples." Old English *cnoll* (hilltop) from Early Modern Dutch *knolle* (clump of turf, turnip).

10. **hew**—B: To chop; hack; as, "a block of *hewn* granite." To *"hew* to the line" is to conform precisely. Old English *heawan*.

11. **churn**—A: To stir vigorously as in making butter. Also, to act frantically; as, "1500 newsmen who will *churn* out reams of copy." Middle English *chyrne* from Old English *cyrnel* (kernel), owing to the granular look of cream as it turns into butter.

12. **daft**—C: Silly; out of one's mind. "Is Dali genuinely *daft*, or is it all one great surrealist put-on?" Middle English *dafte* (stupid, gentle).

13. **shard**—D: Residue; fragment; as, *"Shards* of ice loosen, crunch and mutter." Old English *sceran* (to cut).

14. **bleak**—B: Dreary; dismal. "The prospects for working women are not unrelievedly *bleak*." Also, cold; harsh. Middle English *bleke* (pale).

15. **laud**—B: To praise; extol. "Many homemakers *laud* women's lib." Latin *laudare* (to praise).

16. **spawn**—D: To produce in large numbers; give birth to; as, "funds sizable enough to *spawn* a significant nursing-home industry." Also eggs of fishes. Latin *expandere* (to expand).

17. **cult**—C: Sect; unorthodox religion. "The *cults* are tightly controlled by a leadership cloaked in mystery." Latin *cultus* (care, cultivation).

18. **brunt**—A: The full or main impact; shock. "I have experienced the full *brunt* of the race problem." Akin to Old Norse *bruni* (heat, fire).

19. **scope**—B: Range of thoughts; purview. "The *scope* of what I learned is both enlightening and intriguing." Greek *skopos* (watcher, goal).

20. **brash**—A: Impetuous; giving little thought to consequences. "As long as some of these *brash* Arab countries can pick on Israel, they don't have time to pick on Iran." Perhaps a blend of *bold* or *brassy* and *rash*.

VOCABULARY RATINGS

20—18 correct ....master (exceptional)
17—13 correct .... player (excellent)
12—9 correct ....novice (good)

The Man Who Wrote Moby Dick

The life of Herman Melville, one of the most original of American authors, was as full of drama and tragedy as any portrayed in his books

By MAX EASTMAN

On September 28, 1891, an old man died quietly at 104 East 26th Street, New York City. He had been living there for 28 years, earning his living as a customs inspector. His death received three lines of notice in one newspaper.

Today, his name, Herman Melville, is one of the most famous in American literature. The libraries hold not only his books but books about him. When first published in 1851, *Moby Dick*, his principal work, was so neglected that for the rest of his life Melville thought of himself as a failure. It was published again in 1921, 30 years after he died, and began gathering praise and acclaim. Its sales are now climbing toward the millions.

How shall we explain this literary death and resurrection? There are two answers. In one sense Melville's masterpiece was 70 years ahead of its time. In another, it was 340 years out-of-date.

As a young man, Melville wanted to get free of respectable conventions and live a life of his own. When his father lost the family wealth, and Herman had to leave school, he tried working in his brother's hat store in Troy, N.Y., hoeing potatoes on his uncle's farm near Pittsfield, Mass., clerking in a New York bank. Then he turned up on the New York waterfront and signed on as a sailor on a ship bound for Liverpool. He was 17, and his wages were three dollars a month.

He had health and muscle and a willing mind, but he didn't like the filth and vulgarity of life in the forecastle. He didn't like the food he had to eat. "I never saw the cook wash but once," he remembered, "and that was at one of his own soup pots one dark night when he thought no one saw him." When he got home from that disappointing adventure, Melville taught school, but he didn't like that either; after 3½ years of indecision, he made up his mind to try the sea again.

Throwing a razor and an extra shirt and pants into a carpetbag, he tramped over to New Bedford and took ship on a whaling vessel bound for the South Pacific. Through ill luck he picked a ship on which the living conditions were infinitely worse than on the trip to Liverpool. The captain was brutal; the horsemeat was flyblown; the biscuits were softened only by wormholes. The sailors, with one exception, were unsociable roughnecks. The exception was a boy named Tobias Green. He and Herman formed a friendship, and when after 15 months of whaling the ship put in for repairs at an island in the Marquesas called Nukuheva, they decided to desert.

They took nothing with them but the shirts on their backs, into which they shoved a handful of biscuits and some tobacco. After five days of climbing, and near starving on sweat-soaked hardtack, they came upon a beautiful mountain valley. They had been warned against this valley; it was inhabited by a notorious cannibal tribe called the Typees. But to their surprise the cannibals, after some initial suspicion, welcomed them and treated them—so at least it appeared—not as prospective viands but as honored guests.

During the climb Herman had developed a painful swelling in his leg. The Typee chief, who had taken a great liking to him, did not object when they proposed that Tobias go down to the harbor and see if he could find a doctor.

Tobias never came back; he was shanghaied by another whaler. So Herman lived alone for some weeks in a state of indulgent captivity with those cannibals. They gave him shelter and a servant; they gave him the best of their food; they gave him the prettiest of their flower-decked daughters as playmates.

Herman was a handsome, strong, magnetic youth, and the savages seem to have regarded him as a sort of heavenly visitation to be cherished and preserved. He on his side experienced a feeling not dissimilar to love for his naked hosts. In particular he loved a lithe young girl named Fayaway, with whom he went swimming and canoeing and wandering in the woods. One day in the canoe, to help him paddle, she took off a loose-hanging robe of bark cloth—the only thing she had on—and "spreading it out like a sail, stood erect with upraised arms in the head of the canoe.

"A prettier little mast than Fayaway made," Melville wrote, "was never shipped aboard of any craft."

That romance between a gifted young American and a girl cannibal on an unexplored island in the South Pacific might have been one of the most readable things in our literature if it had been frankly written about. But in the years 1845–50 the idea of putting such realities in a book was horrifying. The nearest Melville came to telling what happened was to say: "If the reader has not observed ere this that I was the declared admirer of Miss Fayaway, he is little conversant with affairs of the heart, and I shall not trouble myself to enlighten him any farther."

Among those savages Herman learned that primitive people, left to their own way of life, may be more happy and good-humored than those who have been afflicted, so to speak, with civilization. "One peculiarity that fixed my admiration," Herman wrote, "was the perpetual hilarity reigning through the whole vale. There seemed to be no cares, griefs, troubles or vexations. Blue devils, hypochondria and doleful dumps went and hid themselves among the nooks and crannies of the rocks."

This experience shaped Melville's views of human nature and life's wisdom in a deeply revolutionary way. It kindled a revolt against the decorous piety of New England folkways; it lifted him out of the mainstream of Victorian culture. "I am inclined to think," he remarked, "that so far as relative wickedness is concerned, four or five Marquesan Islanders sent to the United States as missionaries might be quite as useful as an equal number of Americans dispatched to the islands in a similar capacity."

The Typees' hospitality, to be sure, was a little coercive. They wouldn't let him go. They stopped him with imperious chatter when he tried to pass a certain point on the road to the harbor. Moreover, he kept remembering that this happy dream life might at any moment turn into a nightmare. One day while his hosts were preparing for a feast, he peeked under the lid of a big tub and discovered the picked bones of a human being. Of course, Herman was homesick, too.

He had been there four or five weeks—he remembered it as four months—when the captain of a passing whaler, hearing that an American sailor was a captive among the cannibals, sent a boatload of peaceable natives with a musket, gunpowder and cotton cloth to buy him back. A large troop of the Typees, Fayaway among them, came down to the harbor for the trade. But the Typees, on estimating the value of the goods offered in exchange, refused to give up their precious guest. So, in the midst of the negotiations, Melville jumped into the waiting boat and pushed off, throwing a roll of cloth to Fayaway as he fled.

The Typees rushed after him. Their leader, a chief called MowMow, tried to grab an oar and would have tipped the boat over had not Melville seized a boathook and plunged it into the man's body. He was spared the sight of the cannibal chief sinking in the bloody water, and of Fayaway standing on the beach clutching the cloth, for after dealing that death blow Melville sank in a dead faint.

It is doubtful if the moral precepts learned by Melville in boyhood could render a judgment on this deed of courage and horror by which he got free from his gracious yet savage captors. It made him skeptical of the absoluteness of those standards of good and bad about which people talk so glibly.

He was 22 when he left Nukuheva, and three more years of vagabond adventure intervened before he came home. He was full to bursting with exciting stories when he did come. To solve his economic problems he put the stories into books. *Typee* and *Omoo* enjoyed instant success. With three more volumes that he wrote in the next four years, they earned him enough money to get married on and enough fame to convince him that he was a writer by profession.

Neither the money nor the fame, though, was adequate to

his ambition. He yearned to write something more enduring than South Sea travelogues.

He said in a letter: "Until I was 25 I had no development at all. From my 25th year I date my life." Most of us would put it the other way. Up to his 25th year he lived life to the full. In that year he began to *think* profoundly about life. Later he began to read voraciously—and he found himself more at home in English literature than on the sea. He read Shakespeare and other Elizabethan dramatists and was carried away by their stormy eloquence and their crude, violent gusto.

When he came to write his own great drama, Melville put into the mouths of his characters, as Shakespeare and the Elizabethans did, language that is more intensely intellectual and poetic than they would have spoken in real life. This seemed to his contemporaries clumsy and amateurish. Thus he was as arrogantly old-fashioned in style as he was ahead of the newest Victorian trends in his opinions.

No one knows just when the conception of Melville's masterwork arose in his mind—the drama of an ocean-borne warfare between Man and Leviathan. He dreamed of building into the drama the whole awful ambiguity of the problem of good and evil that had long tortured his spirit. Although almost two years of the life described in his adventure books were spent on board whaling vessels, the terrible enterprise of killing a whale is never described in them. But as a subject for tragic drama, whale-hunting as practiced in the 19th century has hardly an equal in size and grandeur. Beside it, bullfighting is a sport for kittens. And Melville knew all there was to know about whaling.

There was a legend among sailors of a fierce monster of a whale, white all over, known to some as Moby Dick. Melville invented for his tragedy Captain Ahab, a man equally strange and monstrous, seething with rage against that white whale, and roaming the seas with a fixed manic purpose to kill him.

The leisure he needed to write it was supplied by his wife's father who "advanced" him the money to buy a small farm near Pittsfield, Mass. In the autumn of 1850, when the harvest was in, Melville dropped everything and sat down to write his immortal book.

He finished it in a year, and it was published in 1851. But

in another year it sank out of sight. The average annual sales over the first decade came to 123 copies, and over the 25 years after that, 22.

Melville did not stop writing. Even while supporting his family in a clerical job, he managed to put away one story, *Billy Budd,* that, discovered after his death, became a classic. But the great Shakespearean command of rhythms and images was gone. *Moby Dick* had been a burst of genius, and without recognition he could not repeat it.

Seventy years later, and 30 years after his death, a noted English critic announced that he had been induced to read this forgotten book, and that "having done so, I hereby declare that since letters began there never was such a book, and that the mind of man is not constructed so as to produce such another; that I put its author with Rabelais, Swift, Shakespeare." Within a decade, the forgotten customs inspector was recognized as one of the great writers of all time.

Word Power Test No. 14

Canine Capers

By PETER FUNK

Make no bones about it—you'll not be barking up the wrong tree if you fetch the right definitions to these 20 words, which come from *The Literary Dog* (Berkley Books), a collection of famous dog stories. Unleash your imagination and pick up the word or phrase that you think is correct. And don't despair. Dogged persistence pays off! Check your results after this test.

1. **prowess**—A: beauty. B: pride. C: outstanding ability. D: determination.
2. **fidelity** (fĭ del′ ĭ tē)—A: health. B: playfulness. C: delicacy. D: loyalty.
3. **stripling**—A: curtailment. B: a youth. C: exposure. D: a veteran.
4. **sycophant** (sik′ uh fant)—A: coward. B: fool. C: flatterer. D: beggar.
5. **anthropomorphic** (an thruh puh mor′ fik)—reflecting a feeling that animals A: are threatening. B: have human characteristics. C: influence history. D: are good luck.

6. **sinewy** (sin′ ū ē)—A: tricky. B: rowdy. C: strong. D: hungry.
7. **entice**—A: to crave. B: complicate. C: bind. D: tempt.
8. **recant**—A: to retract. B: obey. C: fetch. D: repeat.
9. **provocation**—A: complete attention. B: natural tendency. C: something that angers. D: test of strength.
10. **bulwark** (bul′ work)—A: firmness. B: compartment. C: design. D: safeguard.
11. **audacious** (au dā′ shus)—A: full of energy. B: showing skill. C: pertaining to hearing. D: recklessly bold.
12. **alliance**—A: condition of quiet. B: association or union. C: equality. D: devotion to a cause.
13. **mangy** (mān′ jē)—A: sleek. B: long-limbed. C: shabby. D: voracious.
14. **environs** (en vī′ runz)—A: immediate neighborhood. B: particular type. C: having many parts. D: something that restricts.
15. **refractory**—A: primitive. B: unbreakable. C: trembling. D: stubborn.
16. **transient** (tran′ shent)—A: thoughtful. B: fleeting. C: superficial. D: quiet.
17. **suppliant** (sup′ lē unt)—A: learning with ease. B: able to move quickly. C: filling a need. D: asking humbly and earnestly.
18. **pique** (pēk)—A: to defeat. B: irritate. C: sharpen. D: snicker.
19. **palpable** (pal′ puh b'l)—A: throbbing. B: spreading. C: obvious. D: friendly.
20. **irascible**—A: hot-tempered. B: nervous. C: intense. D: sullen.

ANSWERS

1. **prowess**—C: Outstanding ability or skill; daring bravery. Old French *proesce* (manly courage). "The man boasted of his dog's *prowess*."
2. **fidelity**—D: Loyalty or faithfulness; exactness. Latin *fidelis*. "The *fidelity* of a dog is a precious gift."
3. **stripling**—B: A youth; one not fully matured into adulthood. Middle English *strypling* (possibly "slender as a strip").

4. **sycophant**—C: Someone using flattery to get what he wants. Greek *sykophantēs* (false accuser).

5. **anthropomorphic**—B: Attributing human characteristics to animals. Greek *anthrōpomorphos*.

6. **sinewy**—C: Strong and vigorous; lean; as, the Siberian dog's *sinewy* flanks. Old English *seonu* (tendon).

7. **entice**—D: To tempt or lure by skillfully offering something attractive or desirable. Old French *enticier* (to set on fire).

8. **recant**—A: To retract or reject publicly a former belief or attitude as wrong; as, "The judge would not *recant.*" Latin *recantare* (to revoke).

9. **provocation**—C: Something that incites anger or resentment. Latin *provocare* (to call forth).

10. **bulwark**—D: Safeguard, fortification, defense; any protection against injury, danger, annoyance; as, a *bulwark* against communism. Middle English *bulwerke*.

11. **audacious**—D: Recklessly bold or daring; fearless; impudent; as, the *audacious* Newfoundland. Latin *audere* (to dare).

12. **alliance**—B: Association, union or agreement among countries, or individuals, for mutual benefit. Old French *alier* (to ally). "The dog made an *alliance* with us."

13. **mangy**—C: Shabby; resembling *mange,* an animal skin disease with itching, loss of hair; sordid; squalid. Old French *mangier* (to eat).

14. **environs**—A: Immediate neighborhood; surrounding area; as, "He knew every dog in the *environs.*" Old French *environer* (to encircle)

15. **refractory**—D: Stubborn; obstinate; hard to manage. Latin *refractarius*. "He dragged a *refractory* Pomeranian with him."

16. **transient**—B: Fleeting; passing swiftly; of short duration; as, the *transient* moods of childhood. Latin *transire* (to go across, pass).

17. **suppliant**—D: Asking humbly and earnestly. Latin *supplicare*. "The dog placed a paw on his knee with a *suppliant* gesture."

18. **pique**—B: To irritate or offend by hurting someone's pride; stimulate curiosity. French *piquer* (to prick). "Your bears will be *piqued* at being ignored."

19. **palpable**—C: Obvious; plainly seen or felt; tangible. Latin *palpare* (to touch soothingly). "Charley's bluff is a *palpable* lie."

20. **irascible**—A: Hot-tempered; irritable. Old French *irascible*.
    "The dog was *irascible* in the mornings."

VOCABULARY RATINGS

20—18 correct ....master (exceptional)
17—13 correct .... player (excellent)
12—9 correct ....novice (good)

Seven Words
to Live By

By JOHN W. GARDNER

Suppose that you could offer one word of advice to a young person living in the year 2000. *One word!* What would it be?

Over the past few years I have been asking this question of many friends, and the answers have been remarkably consistent. Three words are almost universally at the top of the list.

The most frequently mentioned word is "Live." It is a sound choice for the First Maxim. If you have in mind Schweitzer's "reverence for life," and a biologist's sense of the complexity and wonder of the life process, you will understand the breadth and depth of the word.

In Thornton Wilder's play, *Our Town,* a young woman dies and discovers that she has the opportunity to live one day of her life over again. She chooses her twelfth birthday. When the day begins, her first reaction is an intense desire to savor every moment. "I can't look at everything hard enough," she says. Then, to her sorrow, she sees that the members of her family are not experiencing life with any intensity. In desperation she says to her mother, "Let's *look* at one another!" And later: "Oh, Earth, you're too wonderful for anybody to realize you! Do any human beings ever realize life while they live it?"

Most people waste life. The First Maxim says, "Live, be aware, experience, grow."

The second one-word maxim mentioned by almost everyone is "Love." People attach many different meanings to the word, and the Second Maxim means all kinds of love—fraternal, sexual, religious, humanistic. But it means above all the capacity to break through the barriers that cut one off from others and from values beyond the claims of self—to give and receive, to commit oneself, not childishly but in mature escape from the prison of self-absorption. It can happen at 18 or 80.

The Third Maxim is "Learn." We're brought up to think that learning is a "duty," and all too often school convinces us that it is a very dull duty. To clear your mind of such nonsense, watch a baby learning to walk. He tries, fails, tries again, improves, bumps his nose, cries, laughs and keeps on. He isn't being dutiful. He's simply doing what he was designed to do—learn.

Many people who suggested the Third Maxim were also saying: Learn who you are, learn to be at peace with yourself, learn the effect you have on others, open your mind to new experience. Learn! It's fun. It hurts. It changes us. And it keeps us "alive." When Oliver Wendell Holmes, Jr.—one of the great Supreme Court justices—was 92, a friend came upon him reading in his library and asked, "What are you doing?" Justice Holmes smiled and said, "Improving my mind."

Live. Love. Learn. Any reader who checks with friends will find considerable agreement on these words. But ask for another choice and you will make a curious discovery: though most people arrive at the same first three maxims, agreement breaks down completely on the fourth. A devout young friend of mine says, "Believe!" A scientist says, "Seek!" A distinguished physician says, "Produce!" I found no consensus.

Then a couple of years ago I was scheduled to deliver an after-dinner speech to the American Philosophical Society, one of the most distinguished scholarly groups in the nation. I decided to put the question to the members and their wives. Where would one find a group of men and women better fitted to assist in the search?

The most popular choice of this group was "Think," although some of them preferred variations such as "Understand" or "Know." The next choice was "Give," and related words such as "Help," "Serve" and "Share." Then came "Laugh," along with "Smile," "Play" and "Enjoy."

Many people have asked what my own preference for the Fourth Maxim would be. My choice is "Try." It's a homely word, and "Aspire," meaning "to try for something better," might seem more adequate. But it's hard to know that what you are striving for will actually turn out to be better. I'll stay with "Try."

Live, love, learn, think, give, laugh, try. Can you pack better advice into seven words?

IT PAYS TO ENRICH YOUR WORD POWER ®

Word Power Test No. 15

An Inventory of Business Words

By PETER FUNK

These words have been taken from the business pages of various publications. Check the word or phrase you believe is *nearest in meaning* to the key word. Answers appear after this test.

1. **course** (kōrs)—A: to search. B: scold. C: move onward. D: direct.
2. **ramification** (ram ĭ fĭ kā′ shun)—A: problem. B: combination. C: reinforcement. D: consequence.
3. **medium** (mē′ dē um)—A: means. B: mediocrity. C: normality. D: function.
4. **ancillary** (an′ sĭ lar ē)—A: important. B: near. C: similar. D: auxiliary.
5. **indiscriminate** (in dis krim′ ĭ năt)—A: careful. B: random. C: partial. D: discourteous.
6. **retrogressive** (rĕt rō grĕs′ iv)—A: moving backward. B: harmful. C: retarded. D: turning about.
7. **supplant** (sŭ plant′)—A: to bury. B: stand by. C: displace. D: work under.

8. **equity** (ĕk′ wĭ tē)—A: credit. B: average. C: example. D: value.

9. **lackluster** (lăk′ lus ter)—A: dull. B: fitful. C: steady. D: obscure.

10. **benchmark**—A: exhibition. B: reference point. C: label. D: repute.

11. **speculate** (spek′ ū lāt)—A: to falsify. B: flounder. C: seek. D: take a risk.

12. **retrospect** (rĕt′ rō spekt)—A: recollection. B: caution. C: secret. D: esteem.

13. **host** (hōst)—A: rivalry. B: unity. C: helping hand. D: multitude.

14. **assess** (a sĕs′)—A: to compare. B: evaluate. C: contrast. D: relieve.

15. **concession** (kon sesh′ ŭn)—A: yielding. B: readjustment. C: prerequisite. D: limitation.

16. **reiterate** (rē it′ er āt)—A: to repeat. B: expound. C: force. D: return.

17. **quantum** (kwon′ tum)—A: formula. B: quantity. C: Indian money. D: space.

18. **magnate** (măg′ nāt)—A: judiciary official. B: person of rank. C: guiding star. D: impostor.

19. **surfeit** (sur′ fit)—A: excess. B: trifle. C: waste. D: haste.

20. **fiscal** (fis′ kal)—A: relating to insurance. B: semi-annual. C: financial. D: medical.

ANSWERS

1. **course**—C: To move onward; run or move swiftly, as in a hunt or chase; pursue; follow close. "Rumors *course* through Wall Street." Latin *cursus*, from *currere* (to run).

2. **ramification**—D: Consequence; result; outgrowth (literally, a branching); as, a *ramification* of the early-closing experiment. Latin *ramificare* (to branch out).

3. **medium**—A: Intermediate means or agency; instrumentality; as, an advertising *medium*. Latin *medium* (middle).

4. **ancillary**—D: Auxiliary; supplementary; subordinate; as, an *ancillary* product. Latin *ancillaris* from *ancilla* (maidservant).

5. **indiscriminate**—B: Random; haphazard; failing to weigh

merit or value in making a choice; as, *indiscriminate* buying. Latin *in-* (not), and *discriminare* (to separate).

6. **retrogressive**—A: Moving backward; deteriorating; declining; as, a *retrogressive* monetary policy. Latin *retrogradi* (to walk backward).

7. **supplant**—C: To displace; take the place of; eradicate and supply a substitute for; as, to *supplant* guesswork with facts. Latin *supplantare* (to overthrow by tripping up).

8. **equity**—D: Value of a property beyond the amount owed on it; as, *equity* in one's home or business. Latin *aequus* (equal).

9. **lackluster**—A: Dull; lifeless; lacking brilliance; as, sluggish, *lackluster* trading. Middle English *lack* and French *lustre* (sheen).

10. **bench mark**—B: Fixed point of reference in measurement (actually, a surveying term indicating elevation); as, the *bench mark* of the year's low prices. Old English *benc* (bench), and *mearc* (mark).

11. **speculate**—D: To take a business risk in hope of gain; buy or sell stock shares in expectation of profiting from market fluctuations; as, to *speculate* in commodity futures. Latin *speculari* (to examine).

12. **retrospect**—A: Recollection; reflective review of past actions. "Viewed in *retrospect*, the commission has rendered a valuable public service." Latin *retrospicere* (to look back).

13. **host**—D: Multitude; large number; throng; as, a *host* of restrictive tax rulings. Latin *hostis* (enemy army).

14. **assess**—B: To evaluate; estimate; appraise; judge the merit or value of; as, to *assess* the needs of the business community. Middle English *assessen*.

15. **concession**—A: Act of yielding, conceding or granting; as, a *concession* to public opinion. Latin *concessio*, from *concedere* (to yield).

16. **reiterate**—A: To repeat; say again and again; as, to *reiterate* a warning. Latin *reiterare* (to repeat).

17. **quantum**—B: Quantity; amount, measurable portion; as, the alarming *quantum* of the national debt. Latin *quantus* (how much).

18. **magnate**—B: Person of rank, influence or importance in a particular field; as, a shipping *magnate*. Middle English *magnates*, from Latin *magnus* (great).

19. **surfeit**—A: Excessive amount; superfluity; satiety; as, a *surfeit* of bad news. French *surfaire* (to overdo).
20. **fiscal**—C: Financial; pertaining to finances of a government or business; as, *fiscal* irresponsibility. Latin *fiscus* (purse).

VOCABULARY RATINGS

20—18 correct .... master (exceptional)
17—13 correct .... player (excellent)
12—9 correct .... novice (good)

The Indian All Round Us

Indian words are a rich part of our language—and one that is too little appreciated

By BERNARD DeVOTO

The Europeans who developed into the Americans took over from the Indians many things beside their continent. Look at a few: tobacco, corn, potatoes, beans (kidney, string and lima and therefore succotash), tomatoes, sweet potatoes, squash, popcorn and peanuts, chocolate, pineapples, hominy, Jerusalem artichokes, maple sugar. Moccasins, snowshoes, toboggans, hammocks, ipecac, quinine, the crew haircut, goggles to prevent snow blindness—these are all Indian in origin. So is the versatile boat that helped the white man occupy the continent, the birch-bark canoe, and the custom canoeists have of painting designs on its bow.

A list of familiar but less important plants, foods and implements would run to several hundred items. Another long list would be needed to enumerate less tangible Indian contributions to our culture, such as arts, crafts, designs, ideas, beliefs, superstitions and even profanity. But there is something far more familiar, something that is always at hand and is used daily by every American and Canadian without awareness that it is Indian: a large vocabulary.

Glance back over the first paragraph. "Potato" is an Indian word, so is "tobacco," and if "corn" is not, the word "maize" is and we used it for a long time, as the English do still. Some Indians chewed tobacco, some used snuff, nearly all smoked pipes or cigars or cigarettes, and the white man gladly adopted all forms of the habit. But he spoke of "drinking" tobacco, instead of smoking it, for a long time. Squash, hominy, ipecac, quinine, hammock, chocolate, canoe are all common nouns that have come into the English—or rather the American—language from Indian languages. Sometimes the word has changed on the way, perhaps only a little as with "potato," which was something like "batata" in the original, or sometimes a great deal, as with "cocoa," which began as, approximately, "cacahuatl."

Sometimes, too, we have changed the meaning. "Succotash" is a rendering of a Narraganset word that meant an ear of corn. The dish that the Indians ate was exactly what we call succotash today, though an Indian woman was likely to vary it as much as we do stew, by tossing in any leftovers she happened to have on hand. Similarly with "quinine." This is a modern word, made up by the scientists who first isolated the alkaloid substance from cinchona bark, but they derived it from the botanical name of the genus, which in turn was derived from the Indian name for it, "quinquina." The Indians, of course, used a decoction made from the bark.

Put on your moccasins and take a walk in the country. If it is a cold day and you wear a mackinaw, your jacket will be as Indian as your footwear, though "mackinaw" originally meant a heavy blanket of fine quality and, usually, bright colors. On your walk you may smell a skunk, see a raccoon or possum, hear the call of a moose. Depending on what part of the country you are in, you may see a chipmunk, muskrat, woodchuck or coyote. The names of all these animals are Indian words. (A moose is "he who eats off," that is, who browses on leaves. A raccoon is "he who scratches with his hands.") You may see hickory trees or catalpas, pecans or mesquite, and these too are Indian words. At the right season and place you may eat persimmons or pawpaws or scuppernongs. All the breads and most of the puddings we make from cornmeal originated with the Indians but we haven't kept many of the original names, except "pone."

On a Cape Cod beach you may see clammers digging quahogs, or as a Cape Codder would say, "cochoggin'." The Pilgrims learned the name and the method of getting at them from the Indians: they even learned the technique of steaming them with seaweed that we practice at clambakes. The muskellunge and the terrapin were named for us by Indians. Your children may build a wigwam to play in—it was a brush hut or a lodge covered with bark—or they may ask you to buy them a tepee, which was originally made of buffalo hide but can be canvas now. They may chase one another with tomahawks. And we all go to barbecues.

The people earliest in contact with the Indians found all these words useful, but some Indian sounds they found hard to pronounce, such as the *tl* at the end of many words in Mexico and the Southwest. That is why "coyotl" became "coyote" and "tomatl" our tomato. Or accidental resemblances to English words might deceive them, as with "muskrat." The animal does look like a rat and has musk glands, but the Indian word was "musquash," which means "it is red."

Some words were simply too long. "Succotash" began as "musickwautash," "hominy" as "rockahominy," and "mackinaw" as "michilimackinac." (The last, of course, was the name given to the strait, the fort, the island, and ended as the name of a blanket and a jacket because the fort was a trading post.) At that, these are comparatively short; remember the lake in Massachusetts whose name is Chargoggagoggmanchaugagoggchaubunagungamaugg.

Twenty-six of our states have Indian names, as have scores of cities, towns, lakes, rivers and mountains. In Maine are Kennebec, Penobscot, Androscoggin, Piscataqua, Wiscasset and many others, from Arowsic to Sytopilock by way of Mattawamkeag. California, noted for its Spanish names, still is well supplied with such native ones as Yosemite, Mojave, Sequoia, Truckee, Tahoe, Siskiyou. Washington has Yakima, Walla Walla, Spokane, Snoqualmie, Wenatchee; and Florida has Okeechobee, Seminole, Manitee, Ocala and as many more as would fill a page. So with all the other states.

Consider such rivers as the Arkansas, Ohio, Mohawk, Wisconsin, Rappahannock, Minnesota, Merrimack, Mississippi, Missouri and Suwannee. Or such lakes as Ontario, Cayuga, Winnipesaukee, Memphremagog, Winnebago. Or such mountain ranges and peaks as Allegheny, Wichita, Wasatch, Shasta, Katahdin. Or cities: Milwaukee, Chattanooga, Sandusky.

The meaning of such names is not always clear. Tourist bureaus like to make up translations like bower-of-the-laughing-princess or land-of-the-sky-blue-water, but Indians were as practical-minded as anyone else and usually used a word that would identify the place. Our unpoetic pioneers christened dozens of streams Mud Creek or Muddy River—and that is about what Missouri means. The Sauk or Kickapoo word that gave Chicago its name had something to do with a strong smell. There may be some truth in the contention of rival cities that it meant "place of the skunks," but more likely it meant "place where wild onions grow." Kentucky does not mean "dark and bloody ground" as our sentimental legend says, but merely "place of meadows," which shows that the blue grass impressed Indians, too. Niagara means "point of land that is cut in two." Potomac means "something brought." Since the thing brought was probably tribute, perhaps in wampum, we would not be far off if we were to render it "place where we pay taxes."

Quite apart from their meaning, such words as Kentucky, Niagara and Potomac are beautiful just as sounds. Though we usually take it for granted, the beauty of our Indian place names impresses foreign visitors. But since some Indian languages abounded with harsh sounds or gutturals, this beauty is unevenly distributed. In New England such names as Ogunquit, Megantic and Naugatuck are commoner than such more pleasing ones as Housatonic, Narragansett and Merrimack. The Pacific Northwest is overbalanced with harsh sounds like Nootka, Klamath, Klickitat and Clackamas, though it has its share of more agreeable ones—Tillamook, for instance, and Umatilla, Willamette, Multnomah. (Be sure to pronounce Willamette right: accent the second syllable.)

Open vowels were abundant in the languages spoken in the southeastern states, so that portion of the map is thickly sown with delightful names. Alabama, Pensacola, Tuscaloosa, Savannah, Okefenokee, Chattahoochee, Sarasota, Ocala, Roanoke—they are charming words, pleasant to speak, pleasanter to hear. One could sing a child to sleep with a poem composed of just such names. In New York, if Skaneateles twists the tongue, Seneca glides smoothly from it and so do Tonawanda, Tuscarora, Oneonta, Saratoga, Genessee, Lackawanna, even Chautauqua and Canajoharie.

What is the most beautiful Indian place name? A surprising number of English writers have argued that question in travel books. No one's choice can be binding on anyone else. But there is a way of making a kind of answer: you can count the recorded votes. In what is written about the subject certain names appear repeatedly. Niagara and Tuscarora and Otsego are on nearly all the lists. So are Savannah and Potomac, Catawba, Witchita and Shenandoah.

But the five that are most often mentioned are all in Pennsylvania. That state has its Allegheny and Lackawanna, and many other musical names like Aliquippa, Towanda, Punxsutawney. But five others run away from them all. Wyoming (which moved a long way west and named a state) and Conestoga and Monongahela seem to be less universally delightful than the two finalists, Juniata and Susquehanna. For 150 years, most of those who have written on the subject have ended with these two, and in the outcome Juniata usually takes second place. According to the write-in vote, then, the most beautiful place name in the United States is Susquehanna. It may be ungracious to remember that it first came into the language as "Saquesahannock."

Word Power Test No. 16

It's a Pleasure to Be Heard

By PETER FUNK

Each of the following words has one thing in common—euphony. That is, each word, by its sound or rhythm, is pleasing to the ear. Pick the word or phrase *nearest in meaning* to the key word. Check your results after this test.

1. **adorn** (a dorn')—A: to cherish. B: decorate. C: perfect. D: worship.
2. **barrage** (ba razh')—A: quarters for troops. B: dispute. C: bombardment. D: large boat.
3. **ensemble** (ahn som' b'l)—A: attendants. B: reception. C: deception. D: complete costume.
4. **serene** (sĕ rēn')—A: musical. B: patient. C: happy. D: calm.
5. **pseudonymous** (soo dŏn' ĭ mŭs)—A: pleasantly smooth. B: contradictory. C: deceptively similar. D: bearing a false name.
6. **cuisine** (kwē zēn')—A: overall atmosphere. B: table setting. C: style of cooking. D: light luggage.

7. **élan** (ā lahn')—A: grace. B: verve. C: diffidence. D: arrogance.

8. **bourgeoisie** (boor zhwah zē')—People who are A: fashionable. B: elitist. C: of the middle class. D: thrifty.

9. **lambent** (lam' bent)—A: spontaneous. B: clear. C: curving. D: flickering.

10. **avian** (ā' vian)—A: cave-like. B: airy. C: characteristic of birds. D: pertaining to the jungle.

11. **ensue** (en sū')—A: To change subtly. B: give up one's rights to. C: follow as a consequence. D: accuse.

12. **liaison** (lē' a zon; lē ā' zon)—A: common goal. B: treaty. C: connection between groups. D: isolation.

13. **suffuse** (suh fewz')—A: to spread over. B: bewilder. C: take away. D: distinguish.

14. **languish** (lang' guish)—A: to procrastinate. B: waste time. C: relax. D: become weak.

15. **repartee** (rep ar tē')—A: insulting remark. B: tedious repetition. C: gracious acknowledgment. D: witty retort.

16. **luminous** (lōō'mi nus)—A: clairvoyant. B: shining. C: pale. D: having a fragile beauty.

17. **repertoire** (rep' er twahr)—A: anthology of stories. B: wardrobe. C: range of skills. D: good conversation.

18. **tenuous** (ten' ū us)—A: unsubstantial. B: tight. C: indecisive. D: cautious.

19. **superfluous** (soo per' floo us)—A: flowing. B: disdainful. C: ornate. D: unnecessary.

20. **bizarre** (bĭ zahr')—A: odd. B: exotic. C: humorous. D: colorful.

ANSWERS

1. **adorn**—B: To decorate; add to the attractiveness or distinction of anything; as, "The color patterns of a butterfly wing might *adorn* a summer print dress." Latin *adornare* (to prepare).

2. **barrage**—C: Bombardment; heavy shelling; if you are under a *barrage* of questions, you are under a concentrated attack of words. French *tir de barrage* (curtain of gunfire).

3. **ensemble**—D: Complete costume; clothes and accessories worn for a total harmonious effect; as, to purchase a summer *ensemble*. Also, a group of performers. French.

4. **serene**—D: Calm; tranquil; peaceful; as, a voice at once urgent and *serene*. Latin *serenus* (fair, speaking of weather).

5. **pseudonymous**—D: Bearing (or using) a false or fictitious name; as, "Benjamin Franklin wrote *pseudonymous* ballads and satires." Greek *pseudés* (false) and *onyma* (name).

6. **cuisine**—C: Style or quality of cooking; the food prepared; as, cookbooks covering *cuisine* from Peking to Paris. French (kitchen).

7. **élan**—B: Verve, style or flair as expressed by spirited self-assurance or brilliant performance; as, to remedy El Fatah's loss of *élan*. French *élancer* (to dart, throw).

8. **bourgeoisie**—C: The middle class: as, "Communists proclaim any tactics are morally permissible in the war against the *bourgeoisie*." Old French *burgeis* from *bourg* (fortified town).

9. **lambent**—D: Flickering; shining with soft radiance: as, "The color is green . . . fresh, shimmering, *lambent* green." Latin *lambere* (to lick).

10. **avian**—C: Characteristic of or pertaining to birds; as, "*Avian* courtship involves elaborate rites." Latin *avis* (bird).

11. **ensue**—C: To follow logically as a consequence of what has preceded; come next; as, the book *Jaws* and the *ensuing* movie. Old French *ensuivre* (pursue, follow).

12. **liaison**—C: Close connection or communication between different groups; as, "The negotiator acted as a *liaison* between players and management." Old French *lier* (to bind).

13. **suffuse**—A: To spread over or fill, as with color, fluid, light, feeling; as, "Her mother was *suffused* with guilt." Latin *suffundere* (pour over or beneath).

14. **languish**—D: To become weak; suffer neglect; as, allowed to *languish* in filthy cells. Latin *languere* (to be weak).

15. **repartee**—D: A quick, witty retort; as, "The first rule of *repartee* is better never than late." Old French *repartie*.

16. **luminous**—B: Shining; filled with light; as, a voice stating in *luminous* words the power of love. Latin *luminosus*.

17. **repertoire**—C: Range of special skills; as, a *repertoire* of problem-solving techniques. French.

18. **tenuous**—A: Unsubstantial; slight; thin; as, "The sun continuously emits a *tenuous* gas." Latin *tenuis* (thin).

19. **superfluous**—D: Unnecessary; excessive; more than is needed; as, "I have cut down every *superfluous* expense." Latin *superfluere* (to overflow).

20. **bizarre**—A: Odd; eccentric; extremely different from the usual style, manner, design, color, etc.; as the *bizarre* siege of Train 734. Italian *bizzarro* (strange) from Basque *bizar* (beard).

VOCABULARY RATINGS

20—18 correct .... master (exceptional)
17—13 correct .... player (excellent)
12—9 correct .... novice (good)

The Cliché Expert Takes the Stand

By FRANK SULLIVAN

Q—Mr. Arbuthnot, you are an expert in the use of the cliché, are you not?

A—Yes sir, I am a certified public cliché expert.

Q—Would you answer a few questions on the use of the cliché in ordinary speech and writing?

A—I should be only too glad to.

Q—Thank you. Now, just for the record—you live in New York?

A—I like to visit New York but I wouldn't live there if you gave me the place.

Q—Then where do you live?

A—Any old place I hang my hat is home sweet home to me.

Q—What is your age?

A—I am fat, fair, and forty.

Q—And your occupation?

A—Well, after burning the midnight oil at an institution of higher learning, I was for a time a tiller of the soil. Then I went down to the sea in ships. I have been a guardian of the law, a poet at heart, a prominent clubman and man about town, an eminent—

Q—Now then, Mr. Arbuthnot, what kind of existence do you lead?

A—A precarious existence.

Q—And what do you do to it?

A—I eke it out.

Q—Have you ever been in a kettle of fish?

A—Oh, yes. In a pretty kettle of fish.

Q—How do you cliché experts reveal yourselves, Mr. Arbuthnot?

A—In our true colors, of course.

Q—And you expect to live to...

A—A ripe old age.

Q—What do you shuffle off?

A—This mortal coil.

Q—What do you thank?

A—My lucky stars.

Q—What do you do to hasty retreats?

A—I beat them.

Q—What kind of dog are you?

A—A gay dog.

Q—And how do you work?

A—Like a dog.

Q—And you lead?

A—A dog's life.

Q—So much for dogs. Now, Mr. Arbuthnot, when you are naked, you are...

A—Stark naked.

Q—In what kind of daylight?

A—Broad daylight.

Q—What kind of outsider are you?

A—I'm a rank outsider.

Q—How right are you?

A—I am dead right.

Q—What kind of meals do you like?

A—Square meals.

Q—What do you do to them?

A—Ample justice.

Q—When you buy things, you buy them for...

A—A song.

Q—You are as sober as . . .

A—A judge.

Q—And when you are drunk?

A—I can be as drunk as a coot, or a lord, or an owl, or a fool—

Q—Very good. Now, how brown are you?

A—As brown as a berry.

Q—Ever see a brown berry?

A—Oh, no. Were I to see a brown berry, I should be frightened.

Q—To what extent?

A—Out of my wits.

Q—How fit are you?

A—I'm as fit as a fiddle.

Q—How do you wax?

A—I wax poetic.

Q—How about the fate of Europe?

A—It is hanging in the balance.

Q—What happens to landscapes?

A—Landscapes are dotted.

Q—How are you attired in the evening?

A—Faultlessly.

Q—What kind of precision and order are you partial to?

A—Clocklike precision and apple-pie order.

Q—When you travel, what do you combine?

A—I combine business with pleasure.

Q—And you are destined . . .

A—To go far.

Q—And what is it you save?

A—Wear and tear.

Q—What goes with "pure"?

A—Simple.

Q—The word "sundry"?

A—Divers.

Q—What are ranks?

A—Ranks are serried. Structures are imposing. Spectacles are colorful.

Q—Thank you, Mr. Arbuthnot. What kind of beauties do you like?

A—Raving beauties.

Q—How generous are you?

A—I am generous to a fault.

Q—How is corruption these days?

A—Oh, rife, as usual.

Q—What time is it?

A—It is high time.

Q—How do you point?

A—I point with pride, I view with alarm, and I yield to no man.

Q—What do you pursue?

A—The even tenor of my way.

Q—What do you throw—and where?

A—I throw caution to the winds.

Q—As a cliché-user, have you any pets?

A—Yes, I have pet aversions.

Q—Any tempests?

A—Oh, yes. In teapots. In china shops I have bulls.

Q—What kind of cunning do you affect, Mr. Arbuthnot?

A—Low, animal cunning.

Q—And when you are taken, you are taken...

A—Aback.

Q—I see. Well, Mr. Arbuthnot, I think that everyone who has listened to you here today will be a better cliché-user for having heard you. Thank you very, very much.

A—Thank *you*. It's been a pleasure, I assure you, and I was only too glad to oblige.

Double Word Power Test No. 1

Words to Appreciate and Implement

By PETER FUNK

In this list of verbs beginning with *a-* or *im-*, check the word or phrase you believe is *nearest in meaning* to the key word. Answers appear at the end of this test.

1. **ascribe** (a skrīb′)—A: to engrave. B: attribute. C: sign. D: write.
2. **imperil** (im pair′ il)—A: to threaten. B: endanger. C: undermine. D: frighten.
3. **aver** (a ver′)—A: to balk at. B: declare. C: turn away. D: postpone.
4. **implement** (im′ plĕ ment)—A: to displace. B: entangle. C: carry out. D: guide.
5. **abscond** (ab skond′)—A: to depart secretly. B: yield. C: abdicate. D: resign.
6. **immolate** (im′ o lāt)—A: to surround. B: baptize. C: vandalize. D: sacrifice.
7. **abrade** (a brād′)—A: to twist. B: unravel. C: scold. D: wear away.

8. **impair** (im pair′)—A: to weaken. B: mend. C: entreat. D: corrupt.

9. **abate** (a bāt′)—A: to tease. B: lessen. C: suppress. D: give way.

10. **improvise** (im′ pro vīz)—A: to plan. B: impose. C: perfect. D: prepare hastily.

11. **abound** (a bound′)—A: to be plentiful. B: tie up. C: bounce. D: spread out.

12. **impede** (im pēd′)—A: to encourage. B: hinder. C: speed up. D: stutter.

13. **affix** (a fiks′)—A: to complete. B: withstand. C: fasten to. D: repair.

14. **impart** (im part′)—A: to bribe. B: separate. C: disclose. D: be fair.

15. **abet** (a bet′)—A: to wager. B: reduce in volume. C: encourage. D: haggle.

16. **impugn** (im pūn′)—A: to attribute. B: attack verbally. C: press. D: hold back by force.

17. **accord** (a kord′)—A: to address. B: grant. C: take note of. D: respect.

18. **impale** (im pāl′)—A: to terrify. B: entrap. C: transfix. D: summon for jury duty.

19. **adduce** (a dūs′)—A: to cite. B: solve. C: persuade. D: compute.

20. **impeach** (im pēch′)—A: to accuse. B: remove from office. C: jail. D: slander.

21. **abut** (a but′)—A: to strike. B: border on. C: cut. D: protrude.

22. **impound** (im pound′)—A: to break up. B: haggle. C: hammer in. D: confiscate.

23. **alert** (a lert′)—A: to warn. B: be quick. C: provoke. D: deceive.

24. **impel** (im pel′)—A: to direct. B: urge forward. C: enliven. D: ward off.

25. **assail** (a sāl′)—A: to attack. B: estimate. C: scale. D: indict.

26. **immunize** (im′ ū nīz)—A: to protect against disease. B: benumb. C: render mute. D: sterilize.

27. **avert** (a vert′)—A: to surrender. B: oppose. C: prevent. D: affirm.

28. **impend** (im pend′)—A: to rely. B: ponder. C: menace. D: reflect.

29. **abash** (a bash′)—A: to insult. B: be shy. C: revel. D: disconcert.

30. **immerse** (ĭ mers′)—A: to conceal. B: float. C: saturate. D: plunge into.
31. **assert** (a sert′)—A: to agree. B: claim. C: imply. D: boast.
32. **implant** (im plant′)—A: to inculcate. B: till. C: hybridize. D: transplant.
33. **amend** (a mend′)—A: to alter. B: suggest. C: bring together. D: subscribe.
34. **impoverish** (im pov′ er ish)—A: to oppress. B: be unthrifty. C: punish. D: make poor.
35. **abstain** (ab stān′)—A: to separate. B: ignore. C: refrain. D: frustrate.
36. **imply** (im plī′)—A: to weave. B: express indirectly. C: set in motion. D: explain.
37. **advert** (ad vert′)—A: to turn against. B: chance. C: circumvent. D: refer.
38. **immure** (ĭ mūr′)—A: to calm. B: harden. C: wall in. D: oppose.
39. **abide** (a bīd′)—A: to loaf. B: approve. C: endure. D: suspend.
40. **importune** (im por tūn′)—A: to beg. B: delay. C: hesitate. D: persuade.

ANSWERS

1. **ascribe**—B: To attribute; consider as belonging to or resulting from; as, to *ascribe* a headache to faulty eyeglasses. Latin *ascribere*.
2. **imperil**—B: To endanger; expose to the risk of injury, damage or destruction; as, to imperil constitutional government. Latin *in-* (in), and *periculum* (peril).
3. **aver**—B: To declare positively; assert in pleading; as, to *aver* one's innocence. Latin *ad-* (to), and *verus* (true).
4. **implement**—C: To carry out; put into effect; to ensure fulfillment by specific enforcement measures; as, to *implement* anti-pollution ordinances. Latin *implere* (to fill up).
5. **abscond**—A: To depart suddenly and secretly; go into hiding, as from the law. Latin *abscondere* (to hide away).
6. **immolate**—D: To offer in sacrifice; as, to *immolate* oneself for a cause. Latin *immolare* (to sacrifice).
7. **abrade**—D: To wear away by friction; irritate by rubbing

or scraping; as, to *abrade* the skin. Latin *abradere* (to scrape off).

8. **impair**—A: To weaken; diminish in quantity, value or strength; as, to *impair* health. Middle French *empeirer*.

9. **abate**—B: To lessen; reduce in amount or intensity; lower; as, to *abate* a tax assessment. Old French *abattre* (to beat down).

10. **improvise**—D: To prepare hastily; arrange on the spot; as, to *improvise* accommodations for tornado survivors. Latin *in-* (not), and *providere* (to see ahead).

11. **abound**—A: To be plentiful; grow or exist in abundance; as, "Fish *abound* in that lake." Latin *abundare* (to overflow).

12. **impede**—B: To hinder; obstruct; as, to *impede* economic recovery. Latin *impedire* (literally, to entangle the feet).

13. **affix**—C: To fasten to; attach; add; append; as, to *affix* a signature to a letter. Latin *affigere*.

14. **impart**—C: To disclose; reveal; communicate the knowledge of; as, to *impart* confidential information. Latin *impartire* (to communicate).

15. **abet**—C: To encourage; assist or support, often in wrongdoing; as, to *abet* illegal gambling. Middle French *abeter* (to bait).

16. **impugn**—B: To attack with words; assail or oppose as false; as, to *impugn* someone's loyalty. Latin *impugnare* (to attack).

17. **accord**—B: To grant or bestow as suitable or proper; allow; award; as, to *accord* the visitor an honor guard. Old French *acorder*.

18. **impale**—C: To transfix; pierce through with a pointed weapon; torture or kill by fixing on a sharp stake. Middle French *empaler*.

19. **adduce**—A: To cite or allege; bring forward as pertinent or conclusive; as, to *adduce* new evidence. Latin *adducere* (to lead to).

20. **impeach**—A: To accuse; charge; especially, to charge a public official with misconduct in office; also, to call in question; as, to *impeach* one's motives. Latin *impedicare* (to fetter).

21. **abut**—B: To border on; touch; as, "The property seemed to *abut* the road." Middle English *abutten*.

22. **impound**—D: To confiscate; seize and hold in the custody

of the law; as, to *impound* stolen goods; also, to collect, as water in a reservoir. Old English *pund* (enclosure).

23. **alert**—A: To warn; call to readiness; as, to *alert* the Civil Air Patrol. Italian *all'erta* (on the watch).

24. **impel**—B: To urge or drive forward; move to action; as, to *impel* workers to greater effort. Latin *impellere* (to drive on).

25. **assail**—A: To attack with physical force, or verbally with censure or abuse; as, to *assail* the witness's credibility. Latin *assilire* (to leap upon).

26. **immunize**—A: To protect against disease, especially a specific disease; as, to *immunize* a person against typhus. Latin *immunis*.

27. **avert**—C: To prevent; ward off; avoid by turning aside; as, to *avert* a quarrel. Latin *avertere* (to turn from).

28. **impend**—C: To menace; hover threateningly; be about to occur; as, a forecast of *impending* storm. Latin *impendere* (to hang over).

29. **abash**—D: To disconcert; embarrass; destroy the self-confidence of; as, to *abash* defense counsel. Middle French *esbair* (to astonish).

30. **immerse**—D: To plunge into something, as a fluid; engross; as, to *immerse* oneself in a novel. Latin *immergere* (to merge into).

31. **assert**—B: To state or claim positively; as, to *assert* one's rights. Latin *asserere*.

32. **implant**—A: To inculcate; impress in the mind or consciousness; also, to fix securely in living tissue so as to induce organic union and growth; as, to implant *artificial* teeth.

33. **amend**—A: To alter or modify; improve; correct; as, to *amend* the rules. Latin *emendare*.

34. **impoverish**—D: To make poor; deprive of strength, richness or fertility; deplete; as, to *impoverish* the soil. Middle French *empovrir*.

35. **abstain**—C: To refrain from action; hold back from participation; as, to *abstain* from voting; also, to forbear; as, to *abstain* from eating certain foods. Latin *abstinere*.

36. **imply**—B: To express indirectly; suggest; as, his behavior seemed to *imply* his guilt. Latin *implicare* (to entangle).

37. **advert**—D: To refer; direct attention; pay heed; as, to *advert* to unimpeachable sources. Latin *advertere* (to turn to).

38. **immure**—C: To wall in; shut up; imprison; as, to *immure* the troublemakers in solitary confinement. Latin *in-* (in), and *murus* (wall).

39. **abide**—C: To endure; bear patiently; accept; as, to *abide* misfortune. Old English *abidan* (to await).

40. **importune**—A: To beg or solicit persistently or annoyingly; as, to *importune* someone to donate money to a cause. Middle French *importun*.

VOCABULARY RATINGS

40—36 correct ....master (exceptional)
35—26 correct .... player (excellent)
25—18 correct ....novice (good)

Cheap Shots and Low Profiles

By WILL STANTON

It was Miss Wilmot, my third-grade teacher, who first made me aware how capricious words can be. She had passed out a vocabulary list for us to learn and I was sitting there sulking over it. I had the wrong attitude, Miss Wilmot said—words were friends, keys to a storehouse of treasure. Take the word "excellent." Didn't it call a friendly greeting from the top of a paper?

No, it didn't, as Miss Wilmot should have known better than anybody. The only "excellent" I saw was on Rosemary Gilmore's paper, held up so I could see it over her shoulder. "Somebody Ought to Try Harder" was the greeting I got from my paper. Friends like these I could get along without.

My experience with words has been that they would just as soon louse you up as not. For instance, all through grammar school I wore tennis shoes. So did my friends. None of us played tennis. Now everybody I know plays tennis. They wear sneakers. See?

Lately, though, words seem to be trying harder. I think they *want* to be nicer. Like referring to old folks as "golden agers." Or when somebody backs his trailer into the grape arbor you say he's "counterproductive." This avoids hurting his feelings and has a dignified ring that "bonehead" does not.

I first noticed how helpful words could be when Congress was investigating everybody during Watergate and the witnesses were all talking about "that point in time." If they'd said "the middle of March" or "Tuesday the 14th," some might have felt twinges of guilt—because at those particular times somebody was supposed to be minding the store. But "that point in time" had no connection; it was sort of floating around back there, and nobody could say for sure just who was supposed to be in charge.

In general, government expressions are very helpful for defensive purposes. Even the kids pick them up. Take the time Maggie's cut-glass pitcher got broken by somebody dribbling a basketball in the house. She finally located Roy under the bed in the guest room. He said he didn't do it. Then how come he was hiding? Roy said he wasn't hiding, just "keeping a low profile."

It's been years, I guess, since any kid bragged that his old man could lick your old man. Fathers today play a "supportive" role. When Roy got into a fight with the Rafferty boy next door, I went over and told Rafferty he'd better teach his kid some manners or he'd be in big trouble. "Oh, yeah?" said Rafferty, a sloping-browed, overly supportive sort of fellow. "That would be the day," he said, hunching his shoulders. By that time the two kids were playing catch, so I decided I'd been supportive enough and went home.

In the old days this might well have degenerated into a neighborhood rough-and-tumble, but nowadays the situation "polarizes." I got up at 5 a.m. Sunday, started the mower and "polarized" the side lawn next to Rafferty's. About 6:30 Rafferty "polarized" a pail of garbage over our hedge. And that was it. Neighborhood life has become much more civilized than it used to be.

I'm not sure when, but somewhere along the line certain books and movies stopped being sexy and started being adult. I know when I was a boy we considered anything "mature" or "adult" to be about as dull as you could get. It was only after I had become mature and adult myself that the words took on a new meaning. But by then I was more interested in herb growing and bird calls.

The word "death" has always been embarrassing to those who have to live with it—like insurance companies. Now they have come up with the term "demise," which is much more pleasant. "Death" is so finalizing. When you say someone has met his "demise" it seems as if he's not really dead, just gone to Philadelphia for a while.

Another helpful word is "life-style." It covers all the things we used to mean by wild oats. Only, wild oats had a cutoff point, age 20 or thereabouts. "Life-style" is open-ended. From today's point of view, Genghis Khan and Attila the Hun weren't any worse than anybody else; they had different life-styles, is all.

The expression "cheap shot" is one that has given the old family quarrel a new dimension. It used to be that when the other person had all the facts and all the logic, you didn't stand much chance of winning. Now you just sit back, let him give his best argument and then tell him it's a "cheap shot."

I was having an argument with Maggie the other evening. She seemed to feel I'd been paying too much attention to a certain young lady at a party. A young lady, as it happened, with vital statistics that would knock your eye out. I explained that I was only being polite. "That happens to be my life-style."

"There were plenty of thin women you could have practiced your life-style on," she said. It was plain the discussion was about to become polarized. No matter what I might say she could accuse me of taking a cheap shot, and I would be a demised duck. I decided to keep a low profile.

"Maggie," I said, "let's settle this in an adult, mature fashion."

She said she was sorry, she had a headache, and went to bed.

I've been thinking it over and I've come to the conclusion that Miss Wilmot was right. Words *can* be your friends. It's just that you can't trust your friends anymore.

Double Word Power Test No. 2

Words of Two Famous Women

By PETER FUNK

Eleanor Roosevelt and Anne Morrow Lindbergh, both especially gifted writers, used the following words in their autobiographies. Pick the word or phrase you believe is nearest in meaning to the key word. Answers appear after this test.

1. **mere** (mēr)—A: humble. B: incomplete. C: only. D: inferior.
2. **interpolate** (in tur′ pō lāt)—A: to flee. B: explain. C: reverse. D: insert.
3. **unequivocal** (un ē kwĭv′ ō k′l)—A: fearless. B: unmistakable. C: incomparable. D: variable.
4. **domestic** (dō mĕs′ tĭk)—A: exclusive. B: native. C: inactive. D: exotic.
5. **mesh**—A: to combine harmoniously. B: squeeze or crush. C: include. D: mix haphazardly.
6. **bolster** (bōl′ stur)—A: to brag. B: rest on. C: support. D: straddle.

7. **damask** (dam' usk)—A: a costume. B: disguise. C: screen. D: fabric.

8. **garrulous** (gar' ū lus)—A: affable. B: noisy. C: quarrelsome. D: talkative.

9. **desultory** (des' 'l tōr ē)—A: disconnected. B: thoughtless. C: slanderous. D: concentrated.

10. **plenary** (plē' nuh rē, plĕn' uh rē)—A: timely. B: combined. C: florid. D: full.

11. **dither**—A: concern. B: exasperation. C: calm scrutiny. D: flustered excitement.

12. **caparison** (kă păr' ĭ son)—A: to adorn. B: leap out. C: contrast. D: strengthen.

13. **covenant** (kŭv' uh nunt)—A: prayer. B: garden. C: agreement. D: debate.

14. **declaim** (dē klām')—A: to denounce. B: clarify. C: refuse to acknowledge. D: speak rhetorically and dramatically.

15. **omnipresent**—A: all-knowing. B: ubiquitous. C: threatening. D: hovering.

16. **distaff** (dis' taf)—relating to A: aides. B: separation. C: women. D: a flower.

17. **sedate** (si dāt')—A: shy. B: impressive. C: calm. D: melancholy.

18. **unobtrusive** (un ŏb trōō sĭv)—A: clumsy. B: self-evident. C: skillful. D: discreet.

19. **entourage** (ahn tōō rahzh')—a train of A: attendants. B: adversaries. C: decorators. D: gatekeepers.

20. **buoyancy** (boi' un sē, bōō' yun sē)—A: sadness. B: durability. C: cheerfulness. D: simplicity.

21. **envisage** (en viz' ĭj)—A: to visualize. B: inspect. C: surround. D: idealize.

22. **tremulous** (trem' ū lus)—A: domineering. B: frantic. C: inadequate. D: trembling.

23. **encroach** (en krōch')—A: to infest. B: spread out. C: weaken. D: trespass.

24. **whorl** (hworl)—A: excitement. B: rare gem. C: spiral arrangement. D: focus.

25. **inexpedient** (in ek spē' dē unt)—A: shrewd. B: trivial. C: ambiguous. D: inadvisable.

26. **temper**—A: trial. B: mood. C: synchronization. D: extremity.

27. **stigma**—A: summary. B: disgrace. C: obstruction. D: honor.

28. **surmount**—A: to overcome. B: influence. C: flourish. D: estimate.

29. **incognito** (in cog′ nuh tō; in cog nē′ tō)—A: unaware. B: exceptional. C: disguised. D: foreign.

30. **façade** (fuh sahd′)—A: embankment. B: cosmetic. C: building front. D: long arcade.

31. **foretaste**—A: bitterness. B: anticipation. C: strength. D: sweetness.

32. **savanna**—A: grassland. B: harbor. C: garment. D: mat.

33. **fecund** (fē′ kund; fek′ und)—A: fruitful. B: changeable. C: decayed. D: strong.

34. **impregnable** (im preg′ nuh b'l)—A: vulnerable. B: full. C: unconquerable. D: stern.

35. **dross** (drŏs)—A: drudgery. B: thread. C: shine. D: impurity.

36. **balm**—something that A: soothes. B: covers. C: irritates. D: blesses.

37. **centrifugal** (sen trif′ uh gul; ū gul)—A: in the exact center. B: rapid. C: moving away from a center. D: consolidated.

38. **expunge**—A: to drain. B: lie. C: distort. D: obliterate.

39. **copse** (cŏps)—A: thicket. B: box. C: stone hut. D: cloud.

40. **insouciance** (in soo′ sē uhns)—A: impertinence. B: unconcern. C: cleverness. D: humor.

ANSWERS

1. **mere**—C: Only; nothing more than; no more than enough. Latin *merus* (pure). "*Mere* gratitude does not convince us of your support."

2. **interpolate**—D: To insert; to distort meaning by inserting new material. Latin *interpolare* (alter). "The actors *interpolated* political jokes."

3. **unequivocal**—B: Unmistakable; explicit; having only one possible meaning; as, *unequivocal* assurances from our government. *Un-* (not), plus Latin *aequus* (equal) and *vocare* (to call).

4. **domestic**—B: Native; relating to a country's internal affairs; as, *domestic* issues. Latin *domus* (house).

5. **mesh**—A: To combine harmoniously; interlock; as, *meshing*

our public and private lives. (Probably from Middle Dutch *maische*.)

6. **bolster**—C: To support, reinforce or prop up. Old English *bolster* (pillow). "His remarks *bolstered* my own inclinations."

7. **damask**—D: A rich, reversible fabric with an elaborate woven design; as, the *damask* hangings in the study. From Damascus, Syria, where such fabrics were first made.

8. **garrulous**—D: Talkative; tediously loquacious; as a *garrulous* cabdriver. Latin *garrire* (to chatter).

9. **desultory**—A: Disconnected; skipping erratically from one thing to another. Latin *dēsilīre* (to leap down).

10. **plenary**—D: Full; attended by all qualified members; as, a *plenary* session of the U.N. Latin *plenus*.

11. **dither**—D: Flustered excitement; confused indecision. Middle English *didderen* (to shiver; shake). "Our delegation was in a *dither*."

12. **caparison**—A: To adorn or dress in an ornate or rich way; as, the splendidly *caparisoned* officer. Old Spanish *caparazón* (saddle blanket).

13. **covenant**—C: Formal and binding agreement; as, our early work on the U.N. *Covenant*. Latin *convenire* (to come together).

14. **declaim**—D: To speak rhetorically and dramatically. Latin *declamare* (cry out).

15. **omnipresent**—B: Ubiquitous; everywhere at once; as, the *omnipresent* photographers. Latin *omnis* (all) and *praesens* (present).

16. **distaff**—C: Relating to women or to maternal lineage; as, the *distaff* side of the Japanese Imperial family. Old English *distaef* (staff on which wool is placed for spinning).

17. **sedate**—C: Calm and dignified; serenely deliberate; serious. Latin *sedere* (to sit).

18. **unobtrusive**—D: Discreet; not too obvious. *Un-*(not) and Latin *obtrudere* (thrust against). "Marshal Tito was protected in an *unobtrusive* way."

19. **entourage**—A: Train of attendants, associates or followers; retinue. French *entourer* (to surround).

20. **buoyancy**—C: Cheerfulness; ability to recover quickly from setbacks. Spanish *boyar* (to float).

21. **envisage**—A: To visualize; grasp mentally; consider as a future possibility; as, to *envisage* international peace. French *envisager* (to face).

22. **tremulous**—D: Trembling; quivering; timid or fearful; as, to feel *tremulous* in the presence of death. Latin *tremulus*.

23. **encroach**—D: To trespass; infringe on another's rights or territory gradually or stealthily. Old French *en-* (in) and *crochier* (to crook; hook). "Russia's *encroaching* threatens the Baltic."

24. **whorl**—C: Spiral arrangement; having a coiled or circular appearance; as, the *whorled* shell of a paper nautilus. Middle English *whorwyl* (whirl).

25. **inexpedient**—D: Inadvisable; not suitable, useful or wise in the circumstances. Latin *in-* (not) and *expeditus* (unshackled). "Advocating war was politically *inexpedient*."

26. **temper**—B: Mood; frame of mind. Old English *temprian* (blend). "My diary is a subjective view of the *temper* of the times."

27. **stigma**—B: A mark of disgrace; as "Divorce has lost some of its *stigma*." Latin (brand put on slaves).

28. **surmount**—A: To overcome difficulties; conquer. Old French *surmonter* (rise above).

29. **incognito**—C: Using a disguise or an assumed name to conceal one's identity. Latin *incognitus* (unknown).

30. **façade**—C: Imposing front of a building; false or superficial appearance; as, to hide behind a *façade* of bravado. Italian *facciata*.

31. **foretaste**—B: Anticipation; a slight experience or knowledge of something to come later; as, a *foretaste* of war. Middle English.

32. **savanna**—A: Tropical or subtropical grassland, sometimes with scattered trees or shrubs. Originally *zavana*. Spanish.

33. **fecund**—A: Fruitful; fertile; producing in abundance; as, the *fecund* variety of tropical plants. Latin *fecundus*.

34. **impregnable**—C: Unconquerable; strong enough to withstand attack; as, "His arguments were *impregnable*." French *imprenable*.

35. **dross**—D: Impurity; scum of melted metals; waste matter; figuratively, anything worthless. Old English *dros*. "There is no *dross* about him."

36. **balm**—A: Something that soothes or comforts; as, the delicious *balm* of water. Greek *balsamon* (balsam tree having an aromatic resin).

37. **centrifugal**—C: Moving away from a center as if affected by a spinning force; as, *centrifugal* influences that upset our

balance. Latin *contrifugus* from *centrum* (center) and *fugere* (to flee). Coined by Isaac Newton.

38. **expunge**—D: Obliterate; erase thoroughly. Latin *expungere*.

39. **copse**—A: Thicket or grove of small trees or bushes; as, a hillside *copse*. French *couper* (to cut).

40. **insouciance**—B: Unconcern; a calm, carefree attitude; indifference. From French. "Eve Curie spoke with charming *insouciance*."

VOCABULARY RATINGS

40—36 correct ....master (exceptional)
35—26 correct .... player (excellent)
25—18 correct ....novice (good)

Little People and Big Words

By SHERWOOD ANDERSON

On my farm in Virginia is a man who has been there, as farmer, for twelve years. He works hard, trying to make the farm pay its own way. I live there in the summer and wander around America in the winter. I meet a good many people of the so-called artist class—authors, musicians, poets, painters. Mostly, I have found, they are very sour on life.

They think that civilization is going to pieces. Things are not right with our country nor with the world. I gather that of course none of this is their own fault. It is the fault of the people, they say; the people, who are too dumb.

I think all this would be of no importance except that from these men and women come the books and articles that people read. So they influence the thinking of others.

These writers and poets and painters seem to be in a terrible hurry. I find that they do not have much time to make acquaintances outside their own circle. So they can never understand the people of whom they complain. The people are "the masses." They dismiss them with a word.

Not long ago I was walking with a friend along crowded city streets. For an hour he talked of himself, of what a terrible problem life was to him. Civilization, he said, was falling into chaos. Why? He used vague words. "People are too stupid." He spoke of "the people," but he did not mean the hundreds of individuals who passed us as we walked, for he was not aware of them. His ears were filled only with the sound of his own complaint.

We passed a boy and girl and I heard her saying: "You don't want to worry. There've been things worse than this before. We're going to come out all right. Why, if things were all right all the time, we'd never appreciate it!" I saw her smiling at him. The boy's frown changed and I saw him smiling back at her.

"These dumb masses," my friend said, making a sweeping gesture. He had seen nothing but what he had been thinking in his head. "Like cattle! How can you make them understand?"

Another friend of mine is a young poet. I took him with me once to spend an evening with a certain family. They are what is called "middle class." They had heard that my friend was a poet, and so they were a little overawed. For a while conversation did not go easily.

A boy of perhaps 20 came by to visit one of the daughters. He stood waiting for her and he seemed embarrassed, talking too loudly and saying things he did not mean. After he and the girl had gone out together, I was told that they had been sweethearts from childhood, but that lately the girl had been attracted to an older man with a successful business. The mother favored the older man, but the father liked the boy. The girl's sister favored the boy too. "She wouldn't be happy with Tommy," the mother said. "I don't want to see any more unhappiness."

The girl's sister got up and excused herself; she was smiling, but I saw that her face was strained. "I shouldn't have said that," the mother said. Then I learned that the man this other daughter had been going to marry had suddenly gone insane. She was herself nearly half insane with grief. But she had been sitting there with us, covering up her grief, smiling, talking, trying to come back to normal.

"She'll get over it," the father said. "It's hard for her now, but she won't let it beat her."

When we left, my friend the poet asked me what I saw "in dull middle-class people like that."

These are the words we hear—"the masses," "the middle class," "the capitalists." Thousands of men working in the great factories; one word, "the masses," makes them all the same, pigeonholed and dismissed. The people who use the word do not see the lines on their faces; they are not aware of the ideas, the problems, the emotions that make these thousands of faces, these thousands of lives each one different from the other, each with its own strivings and ambitions, its sorrows and joys.

"The people are stupid." But there is no such thing as "the people." There is instead the individual. He can be put into this "class" or that "class," but he does not know it. He remains himself, a man or woman shaping his life, living an adventure, striving for happiness, for decency. He knows what he is striving for. He knows so well that he will die for it, if need be. The good fights have never been fought and won by those who use the big empty words and find "the people" dull.

I used to talk with a woman who worked at a machine in a factory. Her husband was dead; there were two children at home to support. She was not a machine that guided another machine. Her children were going to school; she read their schoolbooks and taught herself through her children's minds. She talked of the machine she worked at. "It is a wonderful thing," she said. "My boy knows how it is made, and he taught me. Some day he is going to make a better machine. I think that is the idea of America. It says, 'Here! There are things to do, things to make better. No one is holding you back. You go out, all you young ones, and learn, and work, and make things better.'"

She was a part of "the masses." Her life was not dull. Her life was joy and adventure.

I spoke of the farmer on my place. He has been struggling for years to improve the half-worn-out soil of my farm. He gains a little, year by year. That poor soil is a living thing to him, a sick thing that he is nourishing and helping back to health. He is a man of few words, but occasionally he talks of what he thinks about.

Once in a while when I have been listening for too long to the big thinkers, I go out to the barn where he is perhaps milking a cow. I talk with him and my mind clears of the big words I have heard, all the complaints and questionings. "This is 'the people,'" I think as I listen to him. "This is what is so ordinary and commonplace." And I wish that I had my friends with me, to listen too. The farmer is talking to me of his life, of the soil he nourishes, of an idea that came to him out in the fields the other day. Then he talks of the people in the neighborhood. The son of the family down the road has come back from an agricultural college, and he has a lot of new ideas. His father pretends to be dubious, and they argue, but behind his son's back he says to the other farmers, "You ought to come and listen to my boy." And the young man nearby, who married the girl no one thought much of, the girl he found in the city; well, it seems he broke his leg and couldn't work, and this girl got out and did the work, and took care of him too. It seems she is a fine girl, after all.

The farmer tells me all this. He makes me aware, if I had never been aware before, that each individual's life is a world of its own. It may be a very little world, compounded of things that would be of no importance elsewhere; but it is separate, it is individual, it has its own color and adventure.

That is the answer to those who say "the masses," "the classes," who use the words that mean nothing. They do not see beneath the big empty words to what is right next to them, to what is all around them, to the individuals who are "the people," to the adventure of their days, the ever-varied texture of their lives, the dreams and hopes that, slowly, they work to make into reality. The words are dead, empty and bitter; "the people" are unaware of them, for the people are alive.

Double Word Power Test No. 3

More Words from *Reader's Digest*

By PETER FUNK

The following test words have been taken from articles in *Reader's Digest*. Check the word or phrase you believe is *nearest in meaning* to the key word. Answers appear at the end of this test.

1. **greenback**—A: money. B: immigrant. C: novice. D: scenery.
2. **zap**—A: to jump. B: confirm. C: strike. D: argue.
3. **homogenize** (hŏ mojʹ ĕ nīz)—A: to adapt. B: consume. C: separate. D: blend.
4. **louver** (looʹ ver)—A: pulley. B: kettle. C: Lothario. D: slatted opening.
5. **irreparable** (ĭ repʹ ă ră bʹl)—that which cannot be A: avoided. B: blamed. C: resisted. D: repaired.
6. **maximize** (măkʹ sĭ mīz)—A: to exaggerate. B: intensify. C: moralize. D: transport.
7. **profligate** (profʹ lĭ get)—A: expansive. B: abundant. C: parsimonious. D: wasteful.

8. **evanescent** (ev ă nes′ n't)—A: sparkling. B: durable. C: fleeting. D: colorful.

9. **retaliation** (rĭ tăl ē ā′ shun)—act of A: repaying like for like. B: impeaching. C: summarizing. D: withdrawing.

10. **debase** (dĭ′ bās)—A: to anoint. B: strip. C: cheapen. D: disqualify.

11. **retroactive** (rĕ trŏ ak′ tĭv)—relating to A: rocketry. B: quietude. C: anticipation. D: past matters.

12. **tempo**—A: brevity. B: time pattern. C: osculation. D: haste.

13. **ironclad**—A: pliable. B: unalterable. C: uncaring. D: untrustworthy.

14. **manifest** (man′ ĭ fest)—A: to earmark. B: reveal. C: insinuate. D: conceal.

15. **elegiac** (ĕlē jĭ′ ăk)—A: happy. B: mournful. C: exaggerated. D: sympathetic.

16. **egregious** (ĕ grē′ jus)—A: varied. B: selfish. C: extraordinary. D: social.

17. **archetypal** (ar′ kĕ tīp′l)—A: saintly. B: typical. C: powerful. D: unconventional.

18. **juxtaposition** (juk stuh puh zish′ un)—A: necessity. B: placing side by side. C: outmaneuvering. D: outward projection.

19. **condone** (kun dōn′)—A: to deplore. B: counsel. C: trust. D: overlook.

20. **inveterate** (in vet′ er it)—A: clever. B: shameless. C: habitual. D: slapdash.

21. **actuate** (ak′ chū āt)—A: to estimate. B: put into action. C: prepare a financial statement. D: present proof.

22. **ambiguous** (ăm bĭg′ ū ŭs)—A: long-winded. B: explicit. C: able to use either hand with equal ease. D: not clear.

23. **fracas** (frā′ kăs)—A: a revolt. B: irritability. C: confusion. D: brawl.

24. **depreciate** (dĭ prē′ shē āt)—A: to praise. B: minimize. C: lessen the value of. D: reject or disclaim.

25. **idyllic** (ī dĭl′ ĭk)—A: nostalgic. B: charmingly simple or picturesque. C: mythical. D: menacingly near.

26. **censer** (sĕn′ sĕr)—A: official who enumerates the population. B: container for burning incense. C: social critic. D: military officer who checks mail.

27. **chronometer** (krŏ nŏm′ ĕ tĕr)—instrument to: A: compare colors. B: detect fire. C: record weather. D: tell time.

28. **amorphous** (ă mor′ fŭs)—A: affectionate. B: formless. C: sleepy. D: distinct.

29. **svelte** (sfelt)—A: smooth. B: gauche. C: slender. D: pretty.
30. **dudgeon** (dŭj′ ŭn)—A: anger. B: prison. C: ingratitude. D: desperation.
31. **rococo** (rō kō′ kō)—A: understatement. B: florid 18th-century ornamentation. C: concrete aggregate. D: embossing.
32. **squeamish** (skwē′ mĭsh)—A: having high principles. B: boldly venturesome. C: easily nauseated. D: noisy.
33. **microcosm** (mī′ krō kŏz′m)—A: vastness. B: bullhorn. C: world on a small scale. D: universe as a well-ordered system.
34. **coherent** (kō hĭr′ ĕnt)—A: logically consistent. B: at the same time. C: harmonious. D: confused.
35. **palatial** (pŭh lā′ shŭl)—A: chilly. B: talkative. C: magnificent. D: sere.
36. **harbinger** (har′ bin jer)—A: forerunner. B: bird of prey. C: soothsayer. D: clown.
37. **inimical** (ĭn ĭm′ ĭk′l)—A: not sensible. B: unique. C: alike. D: unfriendly.
38. **stultify** (stŭl′ tĭ fī)—A: to be foolishly stubborn. B: insist upon. C: shrink down. D: impair or make ineffectual.
39. **expeditious** (ĕk spĭ dĭsh′ us)—suitable under the circumstances. B: easy. C: prompt and efficient. D: superficial.
40. **juggernaut** (jŭg′ ĕr nawt)—A: heavy pottery. B: battleship. C: irresistible force. D: solemn pronouncement.

ANSWERS

1. **greenback**—A: Popular name for U.S. paper money first issued during the American Civil War and usually printed in green on the back.
2. **zap**—C: To strike suddenly and forcefully; kill; as, *zapped* to the ground by an intense, glowing beam. An imitative sound popularized in the comics.
3. **homogenize**—D: To blend into a smooth mixture; make uniform and similar. Greek *homogenes* (of the same kind).
4. **louver**—D: Slatted opening; overlapping strips in a window frame to let in air and keep out rain. Old French *lovier* (skylight).
5. **irreparable**—D: That which cannot be repaired, recovered, restored; as, *irreparable* harm to wildlife refuges. Latin *irreparabilis*.

6. **maximize**—B: To intensify; make as great as possible; as, to *maximize* profits. Latin *maximus* (greatest).

7. **profligate**—D: Wasteful; recklessly extravagant; as, *profligate* mismanagement of resources. Latin *profligere* (to strike down).

8. **evanescent**—C: Fleeting; as, the *evanescent* beauty of a rainbow. Latin *evanescere* (to vanish).

9. **retaliation**—A: Act of repaying like for like; avenging a wrong; as, *retaliation* for rudeness. Latin *retaliare* (to repay in kind).

10. **debase**—C: To cheapen; lower in quality, value or character. "When we *debase* our language, we *debase* ourselves." From *de* (down) and *base* (low, vile).

11. **retroactive**—D: Relating to past matters; effective as of a specified prior date; as, a *retroactive* feature of the Senate bill. Latin *retroagere* (to turn back).

12. **tempo**—B: Time pattern; pace at which a musical composition is played, or of activity in general; as, the *tempo* of modern life. Latin *tempus* (time).

13. **ironclad**—B: Unalterable; difficult to change; as, an *ironclad* schedule. Originally an armor-plated ship.

14. **manifest**—B: To reveal; show plainly and clearly. "Intimacy *manifests* itself in many forms." Latin *manifestare*.

15. **elegiac**—B: Mournful; plaintive; expressing sorrow or lamentation; as *elegiac* music. Greek *elegos*, "song of mourning."

16. **egregious**—C: Extraordinary; standing out, usually unfavorable; as, an *egregious* fraud. Latin *e-* (out of) and *grex* (herd).

17. **archetypal**—B: Typical; representing an original model, pattern or prototype; as, the *archetypal* politician. Greek *arch* (principal) and *typos* (mold).

18. **juxtaposition**—B: Placing side by side or close together; as, the *juxtaposition* of architectural styles. Latin *juxta* (beside) and position.

19. **condone**—D: To overlook; treat an offense as if it did not exist; as, loath to *condone* dishonesty. Latin *condonare* (give away, forgive).

20. **inveterate**—C: Habitual; long-established; as, an *inveterate* routine. Latin *inveterare* (to age).

21. **actuate**—B: To put or impel into action; as, gears *actuated* by the clutch. Medieval Latin *actuatus* (reduced to action) from *actus* (act or deed).

22. **ambiguous**—D: The Latin *ambigere* means "to wander about, waver." An *ambiguous* statement "wanders about" an issue and, unclear, scatters double meanings in its wake.

23. **fracas**—D: Brawl; uproar; noisy quarrel; as, a barroom *fracas*. Italian *fracassare* (to break in pieces).

24. **depreciate**—C: To lessen the price or value of; as, to *depreciate* a nation's currency. Late Latin *depretiatus* (undervalue) from *de-* (down) and *pretium* (price).

25. **idyllic**—B: Charmingly simple or picturesque; full of rustic beauty; as, an *idyllic* cove. From Greek *eidyllion* (short pastoral poem).

26. **censer**—B: Container for burning incense. From Late Latin *incensum* (incense).

27. **chronometer**—D: Timepiece of exceptional precision. Greek *chronos* (time) and *metron* (measure).

28. **amorphous**—B: Formless; as, an *amorphous* mass of dough. This word is virtually identical with its Greek ancestor *amorphos*, from *a-* (without) and *morphe* (form).

29. **svelte**—C: Having a slender or graceful figure; trim; as, the *svelte* fashion model. Italian *svellere* (to pull or stretch out).

30. **dudgeon**—A: Anger; resentment; sullen displeasure; as, in a fit of *dudgeon*.

31. **rococo**—B: Refers to an elaborate, florid decorative style— the vogue in 18th century France. An alteration of *rocaille* (pebble or shellwork).

32. **squeamish**—C: Easily nauseated or upset by something disagreeable; as, to be *squeamish* about cleaning a fish. Middle English *squaymysch*.

33. **microcosm**—C: From the Greek *mikros* (small) and *kosmos* (universe). A miniature world; a small-scale representation; as, "A factory is a *microcosm* of industrial society."

34. **coherent**—A: Logically consistent; as, a *coherent* argument. Latin *co-* (together) and *haerere* (to stick).

35. **palatial**—C: Magnificent; palace-like; as, a *palatial* country club. Latin *palatium*, relating to the imperial palace of Caesar Augustus, which stood on the Palatine Hill in Rome.

36. **harbinger**—A: Forerunner or announcer of something to come; herald; as, a *harbinger* of spring. Old French *herbergeor* (provider of shelter).

37. **inimical**—D: Unfriendly. The Latin *inimicus* means "enemy"; from *in-* (not) and *amicus* (friend).

38. **stultify**—D: To impair or make ineffectual; reduce to fu-

tility. "Years of nothing but menial drudgery can *stultify* a mind." Late Latin *stultificare* (to make foolish).

39. **expeditious**—C: To solve a problem *expeditiously* is to be prompt and efficient. The Latin *expedire* means to free one's feet from shackles; *ex-* (out) and *pedis* (foot).

40. **juggernaut**—C: In India, the idol of the Hindu god Vishnu—known, in Sanskrit, as *Jagannatha,* "Lord of the World"—was dragged annually in a huge cart under whose wheels worshipers were said to throw themselves. Hence, any irresistible, overpowering, destructive force; as, the *juggernaut* of war.

VOCABULARY RATINGS

40—36 correct ....master (exceptional)
35—26 correct .... player (excellent)
25—18 correct ....:novice (good)

Don't Nobody Tell Me!

By H. ALLEN SMITH

Some months ago I was writing a reminiscence of my childhood in the Midwest, and was discussing the glories of transportation in the horse-and-buggy days. Suddenly I found myself stuck. There was a word I wanted, and I couldn't get it.

Back yonder there was a gizmo, or hootenanny, that was part of the equipage of most horse-drawn vehicles. In a buggy it reposed on the floor beside the driver. It was made of metal, probably cast iron, and was round, maybe two and a half inches thick, and weighed, I should judge, around 15 pounds. In its center was a metal ring to which a strap or rope was attached. Whenever a driver wanted to leave his rig, he'd drop the heavy anchor at the curb, by the horse's head, and snap the strap or rope to the bit to keep the animal from wandering off.

I was positive that this portable hitching device had a common colloquial name and that I had heard it many times. Yet I couldn't drag it out of memory. So I went to the reference books.

I tried Roget's *Thesaurus* and *The American Thesaurus of Slang* and some old Sears, Roebuck catalogues. No luck. I searched word books and phrase books and the Oxford English Dictionary. I consulted Phil Stong's *Horses and Americans* and prowled through Sinclair Lewis's novels. I found hitching post and hitching block and hitching rail and hitching rack—but no word describing my iron platter.

Now I began talking to myself, as I lay in bed at night, experimenting with letter combinations. Could it have been a crufty? A flonk? Midger? Grawb?

My wife was raised in a little town in Missouri and sometimes can remember things as they were in medieval times. I asked her.

"Oh, sure," she said blithely. "That whatchamacallit. It kept the horse from running away. Now, let me see. What did we call it?"

She stood around and tapped her foot and pressed a finger to her cheek and came up with nothing, so I told her to get back to her warshin'.

That evening I found that my wife had telephoned some people named Williams, who have a reputation for being horsy. Mrs. Williams had promised to call her back. She did, late that night. She said she and her husband and some of their friends had been sitting around, wrestling with my problem. They knew the woffinwhiffle I had in mind, and they had been putting the ends of their fingers together and staring at the ceiling and thinking hard, seeking the word. They had not yet found it.

My wife now phoned another neighbor, Helen Barker, who promptly grew angry with herself because she couldn't get the word off the tip of her tongue, where she said it was. "I've seen a million of the darn things," she said, "and I'll get the answer for you in just a moment." She didn't, so I took over and talked to her husband, Fred, who grew up on a farm in middle New York State. He, too, had seen a million of them.

Fred got to telling me about a freckle-faced girl he used to court when he was a young fellow, and about his buggy and all its glistening accessories. He said it had a patent-leather dashboard, and brass lamps with big red glass rubies set into them, and the shafts were made of ash and varnished, and his horse was a sorrel named Sal and usually wore a rosette at her ear. But Fred couldn't remember the name of the doohickey I was after.

About this time Ira Greer, who brings milk to our house, arrived on the scene. I remembered that he came out of Nebraska, and so I asked if he could think of the word for The Thing. "I'll be darned," he said. "Hadn't thought of that—that—thing in years. Everybody had 'em. Let me see." He pondered a long time. He looks a little like Raymond Massey and does an impressive job of pondering, but this time the results were skimpy. He couldn't think of the name. He went out to his truck and sat behind the wheel a while, and then finally drove off, brow furrowed.

A couple of days later Helen Barker called and said she hadn't been getting any sleep, trying to think of it, so she was writing to a friend in Utica. I can't remember why the Utica woman rated as an authority, but she was.

Then I remembered our old friend Mister Dick in Dallas, an antiquarian of sorts, and decided to splurge by telephoning him. He hemmed and hawed and got talking about whipsockets, and when I finally got him back on the track he said that in the Tennessee hills where he grew up he seemed to remember that they called it a stay-put. I had a feeling that Mister Dick had made that one up on the spur of the moment, and asked him to give some more thought to the problem. Just before I hung up he said, "Could it have been called a hoss-bobbin?"

Soon afterward Ira Greer came to report that he had gone to see a man who used to have a horse-drawn taxi around town. The man took Greer into his barn and showed him one of the dinguses we were after, authentic and standard, and said that he used it nowadays as a sort of anvil on which he repaired broken tire chains. He said that *he* would be inclined to call it a hard-hobble, but that in Scotland, where he came from, they called it a tether-weight. Stay-put, hoss-bobbin, hard-hobble, tether-weight—none of these would do. It had to be something colorful in a short, slangy way. My wife's mother wrote from Missouri that she had communicated with an old horse trainer, who said the term was hitching-iron.

Now Greer telephoned. "I've made up my mind," he said. "I'm going to Nebraska on my vacation. I *know* I can find out the name of it and I won't leave Nebraska till I do."

The lady in Utica wrote that she had scouted the antique shops and the best she could do was the simple word "tether." I called Helen Barker to let her know I had heard from her friend, and she said, "I'd just as soon you'd never brought the thing up. Fred hasn't talked about anything else but that fancy rig he had, and that frump of a freckle-faced girl he was courting. I'm about to go mad."

Mister Dick telephoned two or three times from Dallas saying it was a halter-iron, and then changing to ground-frog, and finally suggesting nag-anchor. Then a telegram came from Dodge City, Kan., sent by Ira Greer. The message: "Boot Hill authorities call it dead man."

I ran into an old friend from North Corolina and asked him about it. He said that down there they simply called it "th' arn."

I was almost willing to settle for that, but not quite. I decided that the thing to do was let matters stand. Everybody was having a good time. I didn't *want* a definitive answer. So, throw out the midger! Cast off the grawb! And *don't nobody tell me!*

Double Word Power Test No. 4

Now You Have It, Now You Don't!

By PETER FUNK

That's the way it seems when you're uncertain about a word's meaning. But once you learn it and then use the word as often as possible, it won't vanish from your vocabulary. Try your memory on the following test. Pick the word or phrase you think is the correct answer. Check your results at the end of this test.

1. **unduly**—A: loosely. B: excessively. C: prematurely. D: willfully.
2. **fossil**—A: bit of pottery. B: sea urchin. C: cave painting. D: prehistoric remnant of an animal or plant.
3. **grimace** (grim′ ăs; grĭ mās′)—A: forced smile. B: snarl. C: disapproving look. D: sullen expression.
4. **fiasco** (fē as′ kō)—A: festival. B: lucky stroke. C: failure. D: misgiving.
5. **xenophobic** (zen uh fō′ bĭk)—A: militantly fanatic. B: extremely cosmopolitan. C: hating religion. D: fearful of strangers.

6. **median**—A: conciliatory. B: tolerable. C: middle. D: thoughtful.

7. **regress**—A: to exit. B: revert. C: apologize. D: reconsider.

8. **doggerel** (dog' ur ul)—A: evasion. B: confused speech. C: satire. D: inferior poetry.

9. **linchpin**—A: gallows. B: lapel jewelry. C: axle part. D: launching device.

10. **sophomoric**—A: frivolous. B: sophisticated. C: obtuse. D: immature.

11. **apocalypse** (uh pok' uh lips)—A: revenge. B: prophetic disclosure. C: unreasonable rage. D: reversal.

12. **forfeit**—A: to defend. B: waste. C: lose. D: agitate.

13. **squib**—A: short news story. B: type of fish. C: quick effort. D: young bird.

14. **ponder**—A: to postpone. B: mourn. C: consider. D: fret.

15. **numismatics** (nū miz mat' iks)—A: auras. B: church rites. C: mathematics. D: science of coins.

16. **restitution** (res tuh tōō' shun)—A: cancellation. B: sanitarium. C: repayment. D: healing.

17. **epoch** (ep' uhk)—A: narrative poem. B: era. C: interlude. D: disaster.

18. **nomenclature** (nō' men klā chur)—A: terminology. B: pseudonym. C. claque. D: title.

19. **globule** (glob' yōol)—A: universal concept. B: foam. C: droplet. D: tinge.

20. **prattle**—A: to interfere. B: waddle. C: shake. D: babble.

21. **levity** (lev' ĭ tē)—A: frivolity. B: evenness. C: mockery. D: great vitality.

22. **chary** (chair' ē)—A: scorched. B: seated. C: bright and joyous. D: cautious.

23. **ambidextrous** (am bĭ dek' strus)—A: right-handed. B: confused. C: two-handed. D: complicated.

24. **refulgent** (re ful' jent)—A: coarse. B: shining. C: fertile. D: diffused.

25. **inimitable** (in im' ĭ ta b'l)—A: unfriendly. B: changeless. C: unlimited. D: unequaled.

26. **sanctimonious** (sangk tĭ mō' nē us)—A: conceited. B: pretentiously righteous. C: solemn. D: dogmatic.

27. **patrimony** (pat' rĭ mō nē)—A: country estate. B: condescending manner. C: inheritance. D: distribution of jobs.

28. **concede** (kon sēd')—A: to acknowledge. B: suggest. C: consider. D: approve.

29. **acidulous** (ă sid′ ū lus)—A: sharp-pointed. B: satirical. C: absurd. D: sour.

30. **elicit** (ē lis′ it)—A: to draw forth. B: break the law. C: beg. D: demand.

31. **desiccate** (des′ ĭ kāt)—A: to chop fine. B: dry up. C: destroy. D: profane.

32. **sardonic** (sar don′ ik)—A: mysterious. B: gloomy. C: scornful. D: sullen.

33. **lachrymose** (lak′ rĭ mōs)—A: enthusiastic. B: oversentimental. C: laughable. D: tearful.

34. **impervious** (im per′ vē us)—A: arrogant. B: steady. C: impenetrable. D: rash.

35. **peripatetic** (pair ĭ pa tet′ ik)—A: walking about. B: frenzied. C: surrounded. D: pensive.

36. **deference** (def′ er ens)—A: shyness. B: respect. C: opposition. D: delay.

37. **officious** (ŏ fish′ us)—A: formal. B: insulting. C: meddlesome. D: authentic.

38. **prescient** (prē′ shĭ ent; presh′ ĭ ent)—A: forbearing. B: foresighted. C: fresh and clean. D: finicky.

39. **stertorous** (ster′ tor us)—A: snoring. B: stuttering. C: loud. D: frightening.

40. **cartel** (kar tel′)—A: topographical map. B: miniature playing card. C: early two-wheeled vehicle. D: combination in restraint of trade.

ANSWERS

1. **unduly**—B: Excessively; improperly. "Security measures were *unduly* lax." From *un-* (not) and Middle English *dew* (suitable).

2. **fossil**—D: Hardened remnant of an animal or plant of a prehistoric age preserved in earth or rock. Latin *fossilis* (dug up).

3. **grimace**—C: Facial expression of disapproval or disgust; as, to make a *grimace*. French.

4. **fiasco**—C: Complete and often ignominious failure. "The birthday cake was a *fiasco*." Italian.

5. **xenophobic**—D: Irrationally fearful of strangers or foreigners. Greek *xenos* (foreigner) and *phobia* (abnormal fear).

6. **median**—C: In the middle; having an intermediate position. "The *median* price of a home jumped by $32,600." Latin *medius* (middle).

7. **regress**—B: To revert; relapse; go back to a former, less advanced state. Latin *regredi* (step back).

8. **doggerel**—D: Inferior, trivial poetry often trying to be comical; jingle. Middle English *dogerel*.

9. **linchpin**—C: Axle pin holding on a wheel. Figuratively, something holding together the elements of a situation. "Freedom is the *linchpin* of democracy." Old English *lynis*.

10. **sophomoric**—D: Resembling traditional college sophomores, immature and overconfident; as, the *sophomoric* antics of our government. Greek *sophos* (wise) and *mōros* (foolish).

11. **apocalypse**—B: Prophetic disclosure; specifically the Biblical book of Revelations. "An *apocalypse* usually reveals God's purpose for the world." Greek *apokalupsis*.

12. **forfeit**—C: Lose a right or advantage by some neglect. "You *forfeit* privileges by not registering." Old French *forfait* (crime).

13. **squib**—A: Short news story often used as a filler for a column. "The magazine printed a *squib* about our musical." Origin unknown.

14. **ponder**—C: To consider something with painstaking care and thoroughness; as, to *ponder* election results. Latin *ponderare*.

15. **numismatics**—D: The science, study and collection of coins, medals and the like. "*Numismatics* can be a profitable hobby." Greek *nomisma* (current coinage).

16. **restitution**—C: Repayment; making good the loss or injury one person has suffered by another. Latin *restituere* (to put in its former place).

17. **epoch**—B: Particular era remembered for important events or personalities; as, the *epoch* of the Korean War. (Greek *epochē* (pause).

18. **nomenclature**—A: Terminology; system of names to classify objects. Latin *nomen* (name) and *calare* (to call).

19. **globule**—C: Droplet; tiny ball, especially a drop of liquid; as, a *globule* of dew. Latin *globus* (round ball).

20. **prattle**—D: To babble; talk foolishly. "She *prattled* on about her problems." Middle Dutch *praten*.

21. **levity**—A: Frivolity; lack of seriousness; unseemly joking; as, inappropriate *levity*. Latin *levitas* (lightness).

22. **chary**—D: Cautious; wary; watchful; sparing in giving or expending; as, to be *chary* of one's compliments. Old English *cearig*.

23. **ambidextrous**—C: Able to use both hands equally well; unusually skillful; versatile; as, an *ambidextrous* ballplayer. Latin *ambi-* (both), and *dexter* (right).

24. **refulgent**—B: Shining; resplendent; radiant; as, a *refulgent* moon. Latin *refulgere* (to shine brightly).

25. **inimitable**—D: Unequaled; defying imitation; unique; as, an *inimitable* storyteller. Latin *inimitabilis*.

26. **sanctimonious**—B: Pretentiously righteous; hypocritically pious; as, a *sanctimonious* politician. Latin *sanctimonia* (holiness).

27. **patrimony**—C: Inheritance of money or property from a father or other ancestor; as, to squander one's *patrimony*. Latin *patrimonium*, from *pater* (father).

28. **concede**—A: To acknowledge; admit; yield to a claim; as, to *concede* defeat. Latin *concedere* (to yield).

29. **acidulous**—D: Sour; acid in taste or manner; tart; harsh; as, an *acidulous* remark. Latin *acidus*.

30. **elicit**—A: To draw forth; bring out; as, to *elicit* testimony from a reluctant witness. Latin *elicere*.

31. **desiccate**—B: To dry up; preserve by drying; dehydrate; as, to *desiccate* apricots. Latin *desiccare*.

32. **sardonic**—C: Scornful; cynical; bitter; mocking; as, a *sardonic* grin. Greek *sardonios*.

33. **lachrymose**—D: Tearful; given to weeping; mournful; as, a *lachrymose* parting. Latin *lacrima* (tear).

34. **impervious**—C: Impenetrable; not affected or swayed; as, a public official *impervious* to pressure. Latin *impervius* (not admitting passage).

35. **peripatetic**—A: Walking about; moving from place to place; as, a *peripatetic* preacher. Greek *peripatein* (to walk up and down).

36. **deference**—B: Courteous respect for the opinions and wishes of another; regard; as, to treat a visiting delegation with *deference*. Middle French *deferer* (to defer).

37. **officious**—C: Meddlesome; overready with gratuitous advice or assistance; as, an *officious* clerk. Latin *officium* (service).

38. **prescient**—B: Foresighted; having knowledge of future events; prophetic; as, a *prescient* economic analyst. Latin *praescire* (to know beforehand).

39. **stertorous**—A: Accompanied by a hoarse snoring or gasping sound; as, deep, *stertorous* breathing. Latin *stertere* (to snore).

40. **cartel**—D: Combination of organizations for the purpose of limiting competition, fixing prices or otherwise controlling production and distribution. French *cartel* (letter of defiance).

VOCABULARY RATINGS

40—36 correct ....master (exceptional)
35—26 correct .... player (excellent)
25—18 correct ....novice (good)

Language
on the Skids

By EDWIN NEWMAN

It is typical of the English spoken on this side of the Atlantic that enough is almost never enough. Cecil Smith, television critic of the Los Angeles *Times,* considered CBS's "Bicentennial Minutes" not merely unique but singularly unique. Sen. Abraham Ribicoff of Connecticut was worried not only about nuclear proliferation but about the spread of nuclear proliferation. And Reggie Jackson, the New York *Times* advised its readers, "stole second successfully," which is better than stealing it unsuccessfully.

All of this is redundancy, to which we have become addicted. A large part of our speech and writing is unnecessary and boring, which makes reading and conversation a chore. We slog through the repetitious, and tarry when we should be moving on. Redundancy triumphs.

One reason for our extravagant use of words is the feeling that an idea is more effective if it is repeated and reinforced. That is why Jimmy Carter once described the international situation as very dormant. (Those were the days!) It is why he said that the place where he would meet Leonid Brezhnev would depend not merely on a mutual decision but on "a mutual decision between us." You can't be too careful when dealing with the Russians.

Another cause is a failure to understand what words mean. The New York *Daily News* would not have said of a motion picture that it "extolled the evils of the advertising business" if it knew what extolled meant. The weather forecaster at the CBS station in Washington, D.C., would not have said, "Tomorrow afternoon, the temperature will gradually plummet. . . ." And what could have led the New Bedford, Mass., *Standard Times* to run this headline: "Tie vote kills bottle bill, but not fatally"?

There is a third reason for our extravagant use of words— a desire to make what is being done, however simple and routine it may be, sound grand and complicated. Thus, two newspapers in Nevada announce that they intend to put up a building. Do they call it a building? No. It is to be "a community-information center." The Postal Service issues statements about "sortation" of mail. Not sorting. Sortation. The Los Angeles City Teachers' Mathematics Association, at its Annual Recognition Dinner, schedules an associative hour rather than a cocktail hour. What does one do during an associative hour? Get acquainted? Not since computer language has descended on us. One interfaces on a personal basis. By the way, if any well-dressed women are present, it is possible that their dress reflects "Executive Wardrobe Engineering."

Why is such language used? Self-importance, of course, but also because it serves as a fence that keeps others outside and respectful, or leads them to ignore what is going on inside because it is too much trouble to find out. So you may hear about "a horizontal analysis spanning the formal vertical departmental structure" intended to "identify multi-purpose citizen contacts requiring timely responses." Or you may hear of a California school district that closes schools not because there are fewer pupils than expected but because of "accelerated enrollment slippage."

This sort of language is increasingly characteristic of a society where engaged couples are said to be in a commitment situation, and where an economist may refer to work as labor-force participation. In Boston, the Metropolitan District Commission did not want to say, "Keep off the ice." It urged that "all persons terminate using any body of water under MDC control for any ice-related recreation." It could have been worse. It could have been ice-related recreation-oriented activity.

There is, of course, a technique involved, but it is easy to grasp. Never say that a tank may spring a leak. Say there may be a "breach of containment." Never say of a product that people won't buy it. Say that it "met consumer resistance." In Knoxville, Tenn., a nurse won a product-naming contest with the suggestion that dust covers for medical equipment be called instead "sterility maintenance covers." That was worth $500 and a lunch at the Hyatt Regency Hotel.

I want to turn now to what I take to be the new pastime. It is "izing." A reporter I know, covering a Presidential visit to Boston, asked the Secret Service where he could park his car. The Secret Service could not help. What should he do, then? "If I were you," the Secret Service man replied, "I would put myself in a chauffeurized situation." The head of the United States Professional Tennis Association proposed "to focalize all major USPTA activities and programs from a single site." Would he be the focalist? Some plastic surgeons, advertising a customized approach, promise "wrinkles youthfulized." This, apparently, leaves the patients with young wrinkles.

Sports broadcasters often have only a shaky grip on grammar and on the connection between words and meaning. During one football game, the announcer told viewers that because of the way some of the boxes in the Superdome were placed, he could not visually see them. This sort of thing is by no means confined to the sports world. For example, we have all heard about alleged victims. They have become confused in some journalistic minds with intended victims, but intended victims are sometimes rendered as would-be victims, who apparently go out in the hope of being robbed.

An ironic thing is happening now. As we demand more and more openness from those in public life—unwisely, it seems to me—our language becomes more and more obscure, turgid, ponderous and overblown. The candor expected of public officials about their health, their money, their private lives is offset in public matters by language that conceals more than it tells, and often conceals the fact that there is little or nothing worth telling.

We ought to demand that our leaders speak better English, so that we know what they are talking about and, incidentally, so that they do. Some safety does lie in more sensible public attitudes, especially toward the public-relations and advertising techniques now widely used by politicians. It lies also in independent reporting by those of us in the news business, and in greater skepticism on the part of the public, and in an unremitting puncturing of the overblown. In all of this, language is crucial.

I have been told that my view is cranky and pedantic, that I want to keep the language from growing, and to impose a standard and rigid English. Far from it. Our language should be specific and·concrete, eloquent where possible, playful where possible, and personal so that we don't all sound alike. Instead, high crimes and misdemeanors are visited upon it, and those who commit them do not understand that the crimes are crimes against themselves. The language belongs to all of us. We have no more valuable possession.

Double Word Power Test No. 5

"All Things Change"

By PETER FUNK

So wrote the poet Ovid. Each test below reflects change—in the worlds of science, sport, fashion or politics. Some of these words are recent coinages, others are old words in new garb. Check the word or phrase *nearest in meaning* to the key word. Answers appear at the end of this test.

1. **clout**—A: moron. B: thug. C: surmise. D: influence.
2. **debrief** (de brēf′)—A: to perplex. B: brainwash. C: relax. D: interrogate.
3. **ploy**—A: humor. B: diagram. C: dishonesty. D: stratagem.
4. **dyslexia** (dis lĕk′ sē uh)—impairment of A: hearing. B: feeling. C: reading. D: tasting.
5. **circadian** (sir kā′ dē un)—having to do with A: insects. B: amnesia. C: premonitions. D: bodily cycles.
6. **troika** (troy′ kă)—A: vigorous dance. B: tri-cornered hat. C: group of three. D: ski maneuver.
7. **clone** (klōn)—A: to duplicate. B: separate. C: manipulate. D: dry.

8. **charismatic** (kă riz mă′ tik)—A: magnetically appealing. B: mystifying. C: clear. D: complex.

9. **binary** (bī′ năr ē)—A: multiplex. B: methodical. C: two-fold. D: essential.

10. **autistic** (awe tis′ tic)—A: alert. B: argumentative. C: creative. D: unresponsive.

11. **blitz**—A: sudden attack. B: skin blemish. C: unexpected storm. D: ethnic food.

12. **biodegradable** (bī ō dĭ grā′ dă b'l)—A: capable of decomposing. B: systematized. C: polluting. D: shameful.

13. **unisex** (ūn′ ĭ seks)—related to A: wheel-less vehicle. B: sexlessness. C: indistinguishability as to male or female. D: torpor.

14. **exploit** (eks ploit′)—A: to clarify. B: overstate. C: dare. D: use unfairly.

15. **byzantine** (biz′ 'n tēn)—A: courtly. B: intricate. C: alluring. D: cruel.

16. **mafia** (mă′ fē ă)—A: poisonous plant. B: religious sect. C: power group. D: antique instrument.

17. **fail-safe**—A: conservative. B: open-ended. C: undecided. D: providing protection.

18. **recycle** (rē sī′ k'l)—A: to reprocess. B: change. C: spin. D: substitute.

19. **waffle**—A: to dispose of. B: ransack. C: be indecisive. D: daydream.

20. **impinge** (im pinj′)—A: to infringe. B: pierce. C: shut in. D: meddle with.

21. **flux**—A: a gradual curving. b: continuous change. C: unexpected substitute. D: shimmering light.

22. **innovation** (in ō vā′ shun)—A: unusual happening. B: new approach. C: respite. D: rejection.

23. **affirm** (ă firm′)—A: to state positively. B: convince. C: make taut. D: deny.

24. **prospective** (prō spĕk′ tiv)—having to do with a A: viewpoint. B: peculiarity. C: sense of proportion. D: future expectation.

25. **resolution** (rĕz ō lū′ shun)—A: firm decision. B: certainty. C: denial. D: self-control.

26. **matutinal** (mă tū′ tĭ nal)—A: motherly. B: clear. C: early. D: trusting.

27. **inception** (in sep′ shun)—A: beginning. B: appointment. C: progression. D: imagination.

28. **neologism** (nē ŏl′ ō jiz′m)—A: looking to the past. B:

linguistic coinage or alteration. C: figure of speech. D: half-truth.

29. **transfigure** (trans fig′ yur)—A: to put an end to. B: combine. C: reorganize. D: change dramatically.

30. **anticipate** (an tis′ ĭ pāte)—A: to contrive. B: ignore. C: foresee. D: ponder.

31. **debut** (dĕ bū′)—A: recapitulation. B: strong point. C: first appearance. D: clever retort.

32. **novice** (nŏv′ is)—A: beginner. B: new star. C: shrewd bargainer. D: fad.

33. **induce** (in dūce′)—A: to meet. B: bring. C: decrease. D: persuade.

34. **renascent** (rĭ nās′ ent)—A: reminiscent of. B: indolent. C: born-again. D: progressive.

35. **germinate** (jer′ mĭ nāte)—A: to sprout. B: multiply. C: sterilize. D: stimulate.

36. **novel**—A: authentic. B: unforgettable. C: refreshing. D: new.

37. **preface** (pref′ is)—A: preference. B: supplement. C: summary. D: introduction.

38. **genesis** (jen′ ĕ sis)—A: phenomenon. B: false authority. C: creativity. D: origin.

39. **odyssey** (odd′ ĭ sē)—A: long journey. B: curious event. C: search. D: great joy.

40. **optimistic** (op tĭ mis′ tik)—A: hopeful. B: strident. C: lively. D: favorable.

ANSWERS

1. **clout**—D: Influence; power; as, having political *clout*. Its literal meaning, a hard blow, may derive from Old English *clut* (small cloth and hence a bandage).

2. **debrief**—D: To interrogate a pilot or emissary just returned from a mission; as, to *debrief* the astronaut.

3. **ploy**—D: Stratagem or maneuver; as, "Many dieters develop their own *ploys* for avoiding snacks." A shortened form of employ.

4. **dyslexia**—C: Impairment of the ability to read or write normally; as, "Millions of bright children are affected by *dyslexia*." Greek *dys* (bad) and *lexis* (speech).

5. **circadian**—D: Having to do with bodily cycles; as, disruption of our *circadian* sleep patterns by jet travel. Latin *circa* (about) and *dies* (day).

6. **troika**—C: A group of three with equal power; as, a *troika* of three vice presidents. Russian (a vehicle drawn by three horses abreast).

7. **clone**—A: To duplicate; produce identical organisms asexually from a single common ancestor such as a cell. Greek *klon* (twig).

8. **charismatic**—A: Having magnetically appealing qualities that inspire loyalty; as, "Churchill was a *charismatic* speaker." Greek *charisma* (favor, gift).

9. **binary**—C: Twofold: involving two alternatives; as, the *binary* code that governs most computers. Latin *binarius* from *bini* (two by two).

10. **autistic**—D: Unresponsive; oblivious to the real world; as, "Autistic children cannot make sense of what they see and hear." Coined in 1943 from Greek *autos* (self).

11. **blitz**—A: Sudden, violent attack; as, a *blitz* of the quarterback by the opposing team. Short for German *blitzkrieg*, from *blitz* (lightning) and *krieg* (war).

12. , **biodegradable**—A: Able to decompose biologically into harmless products by bacterial action; as, *biodegradable* containers. Greek *bios* (life) and Latin *degradare* (to reduce).

13. **unisex**—C: Indistinguishability as to male or female; as, a *unisex* haircut. Latin *unus* (one) and sex.

14. **exploit**—D: To use unfairly for one's own profit; as, to *exploit* a friendship. This critical connotation is displacing the original meaning, to make good use of. Old French *esploit* (action).

15. **byzantine**—B: Intricate and complicated; as, the city's *byzantine* political structure. From Byzantium (ancient name for Istanbul).

16. **mafia**—C: People with common backgrounds in a power group; as, "John Kennedy joked about his Irish *mafia*." Sicilian (boldness) from Arabic *mahyah* (boasting).

17. **fail-safe**—D: Providing protection by counteracting a possible malfunction; as, a *fail-safe* mechanism to prevent a power blackout.

18. **recycle**—A: To reprocess glass, cans, etc., for subsequent reuse. Latin *re* (again) and Greek *kyklos* (circle).

19. **waffle**—C: To be indecisive; vague; evasive; as, "The can-

didate *waffled* on the abortion question." Obsolete English *waff* (to yelp).

20. **impinge**—A: To infringe; collide with; encroach; as, to *impinge* on another's rights. Latin *impingere* (to drive against).

21. **flux**—B: Latin *fluere* means to flow; hence, when fashions or policies are in a state of *flux*, they are going through continuous change.

22. **innovation**—B: New approach; a change in the usual way of doing things. Latin *innovare* (to renew).

23. **affirm**—A: To state positively what one believes to be true; as, to *affirm* one's faith in democracy. Latin *adfirmare* (to strengthen, assert).

24. **prospective**—D: A *prospective* contract is expected sometime in the future; it is likely or probable. Latin *prospicere* (to look forward).

25. **resolution**—A: Firm decision; a resolve on a course of action; as, a New Year's *resolution* to diet. Latin *resolvere* (to unbind, cancel).

26. **matutinal**—C: From ancient Rome's goddess of the dawn, *Matuta*. Hence, early or in the morning; as, *matutinal* prayers.

27. **inception**—A: Beginning: the act of starting and undertaking; as, to be with a project since its *inception*. Latin *incipere* (to begin).

28. **neologism**—B: Coinage or alteration in language: new word or expression; as, much slang is composed of *neologisms*. French *neologisme*, from Greek *neo* (new) and *logos* (word).

29. **transfigure**—D: To change dramatically the appearance, nature or character of something; transform, as, "She was *transfigured* by love." Latin *transfigurare* (to change in shape).

30. **anticipate**—C: To foresee; realize beforehand; act in advance so as to prevent. "Football star O. J. Simpson *anticipates* his opponents' moves." Latin *anticipare* (to take before).

31. **debut**—C: First public appearance; start of a career; as, a concert pianist's *debut*. French *débuter* (to make the first stroke in a game, usually billiards; to lead off).

32. **novice**—A: Beginner; one with no experience or training in a specific field; as, the *novice* carpenter. Latin *novus* (new).

33. **induce**—D: To persuade; influence, prevail upon or lead to some particular action, often subtly; as, "A sound argument *induces* people to agree." Latin *in* (in) and *ducere* (to lead).

34. **renascent**—C: Being born again; showing renewed life, growth or vigor; as, the aging entertainer's *renascent* career. From Latin *renasci, re* (again) and *nasci* (born).

35. **germinate**—A: To sprout; begin to grow and develop; come into existence. Seeds *germinate;* a meeting may *germinate* valuable suggestions. Latin *germinare* (to sprout forth).

36. **novel**—D: New; unusual; strikingly different; as, a *novel* architectural design. Latin *novus*.

37. **preface**—D: Introduction; a statement explaining the subject, purpose and scope of a book, article or speech; as, a textbook's *preface*. Latin *praefatio* (a saying beforehand).

38. **genesis**—D: The origin or beginning of anything; as, "The *genesis* of the strike was a disagreement over wages." Also, the first book of the Bible. Greek *genesis* (creation).

39. **odyssey**—A: Any long, adventurous journey. From Homer's ancient Greek epic poem describing the ten-year wanderings of *Odysseus*.

40. **optimistic**—A: Hopeful; sanguine. An *optimistic* person is one who cheerfully expects everything to work out well. Latin *optimus* (the best).

VOCABULARY RATINGS

40—36 correct ....master (exceptional)
35—26 correct .... player (excellent)
25—18 correct ....novice (good)

Unforgettable S. J. Perelman

Natty and shy, but a master of the English language, he made us laugh for half a century

By PHILIP HAMBURGER

Sidney Joseph Perelman came to dinner at my home one October evening and, as always, arrived precisely on time. Sid was one of the world's great humorists, but he saw nothing funny about being late. He detested many shoddy things in this world, but reserved some of his deepest scorn for those who wrote badly and who were rude. So I was not at all surprised when the bell rang at *exactly* 7:30.

"Sid right on the button again," I said to my wife. I opened the door and there he was, ruddy-faced, as precise in his dress as in his schedule, his appearance belying his 75 years. Although born in Brooklyn, and raised in Providence, R.I., he looked as usual the very model of a modern English gentleman, heading for his favorite London club. He was wearing the small-brimmed porkpie hat that had become something of a trademark the past few years, well-pressed slacks, and a finely woven tweed jacket that certainly came from somewhere in the British Isles.

I knew, however, that this natty get-up was just one of Sid's many roles. He once abruptly departed London, saying that he had become fed up with "too much couth" and was overcome with an uncontrollable desire for a hot pastrami sandwich. Or he would be off in some exotic part of the globe, enjoying its delights, and quite suddenly require the sight of a caraway seed and a piece of rye bread.

Sid started most evenings quietly, and that October evening was no exception. I always had the feeling when I was with him that he required time to collect his thoughts, to feel secure, take private soundings and overcome a monumental shyness. With his regal manners, his silences were immensely dignified. He would cock his head to one side in order not to miss a word of what was being said, and the light would catch the reflection in his granny glasses as he subtly prodded someone into expressing what was on his mind.

But when he began to warm up and speak freely, one could close one's eyes and swear that he was reading from the printed page, so close to his written words were the rhythms of his speech. On the evening in question, he began to speak with great enthusiasm about a recent book of reminiscences of James Joyce (whom he worshiped as "the great comic writer of our time"), then launched into some devastating comments on two writers he felt were becoming fatuous and overbearing. It was a neat, swift job of skewering. He talked about the theater, dwelt briefly on the real names of some old favorite silent-screen stars, and departed with a jaunty wave around 11:30, heading back to his hotel rooms overlooking New York's quiet Gramercy Park. Sometime during the following night he died peacefully in his sleep.

S. J. PERELMAN'S 20 books remain his permanent monument, from *Dawn Ginsbergh's Revenge* in 1929 to *Vinegar Puss* in 1975; his legacy also lies in hundreds of pieces in *The New Yorker;* in *Horse Feathers* and *Monkey Business,* those hilarious Marx Brothers movies; and in his inspired script for the Oscar-winning film *Around the World in Eighty Days.* The London *Observer's* obituary was headed, "Farewell My Lovely Sid"; *The New Yorker* said that "the town grew suddenly sombre: S. J. Perelman, who had been making us laugh for half a century, was gone."

Some of his great lines come instantly to mind: "I've got

Bright's disease and he has mine." "It takes two to tango, but only one to squirm." I cannot forget a dusty old bookshop "where every prospect sneezes, and only Mann, the owner, is vile." I find that the names of his characters will not go away: White-lipped and Trembling, brokers; Howells & Imprecation, lawyers; Umlaut, the *Times* theater critic; Urban Sprawl, the architect; Lothar Perfidiasch, "noted Hungarian playwright and plagiarist"; Moe Juste, the French grammarian; Chalky After-taste and His Musical Poltroons, a ragtime band; John J. Antennae, the radio evangelist, "fox-faced, sallow, closely related to God on his mother's side"; Marcel Riboflavin, the French police inspector in *The Saucier's Apprentice*. ("'In France,' Marcel said with wintry dignity, 'accidents occur in the bedroom, not in the kitchen.'")

His titles will not go away either: "Frou-Frou, Or the Future of Vertigo"; "Boy Meets Girl Meets Foot"; "Caution—Soft Prose Ahead"; "Stringing Up Father"; "The Hand That Cradles the Rock." His influence on comic writing, expressed in these and so many other works, was immense. When he died, President Carter noted that "Like Mark Twain, George Ade, Ring Lardner and James Thurber, S. J. Perelman made a permanent contribution not only to American humor but to American literature as well."

Words, of course, were the mainspring of his life. He played with them, molded them to his desire. Shortly after he died, E. B. White and I had a talk about him. "Sid had the greatest and most formidable vocabulary I have ever encountered," said White, who is one of the great living masters of English prose. "It was like an elaborate erector set, one word leading to another, joined to still another, to produce a truly remarkable structure."

White recalled that Perelman's preoccupation with words often overshadowed even his sense of self. Some years ago, when White and his wife were wintering in Sarasota, Sid and his wife, Laura, arrived in a state of immense excitement. "We were in a dreadful accident in North Carolina on the way down," Sid said. "Damn near a head-on collision." The Whites naturally wondered whether any serious injuries had been sustained. "That's not the point," said Sid emphatically. "When the tow truck finally brought my car to a garage, the garage man took one look and said, 'Your car has been totaled!'"

Sid's voice rose. "Did you hear that?" he asked. "An entirely new word for me—*totaled!*"

PEOPLE were always making a fuss over Sid, especially in bookstores and at literary parties, but he was acutely embarrassed by such attentions. He was an extremely modest man, at his best with a group of old friends leisurely seated around a table in a familiar restaurant.

For many years a group of us would gather weekly for lunch at a seafood restaurant near Times Square. Sid was the generally accepted master of the gatherings, at which there were many reminiscences of Hollywood days. Screen writer Albert Hackett would remind Sid that when all the other screen writers received their pay checks they would solemnly deposit them. Sid would instantly cash his. "Now that we have the 1500 or so in hand," he would say to Laura, "we can go back to New York."

Old friends feel that Sid spent his entire life being anxious about money. He never permitted himself to shed money worries, even when there was small need for concern. He rarely took cabs, and he watched his pennies. He worried in general. He worried, for instance, about packing, and before any trip, long or short, he would pack and repack, arranging shirts, socks and ties in differing combinations best suited to a tightly closed suitcase.

He tried hard to communicate with people outside his inner circle, but it often took a great deal of will power on his part. "He was so crisp and neat and austere," a young woman told me not long after he died. "He seemed almost totally unapproachable until you gained his confidence. From that moment forward, he became a thorough romantic, attentive, observant, confiding. One then felt that one could tell Sid anything, and it would stop with him. He never failed to notice what a woman was wearing, or what jewelry she had put on. In fact, there was little that escaped his notice at any time."

A WITHDRAWN MAN, Sid required considerable solitude and quiet in order to work. He could never write, for instance, in a formal office such as *The New Yorker,* nor did he try. For many years, beginning in the early '50s and continuing until Laura's death in 1970, he rented a shabby room on the third floor of a nondescript red-brick walkup on Sixth Avenue. The tiny room in which he worked had one window opening onto a blank wall. "There is no sky to distract me," Sid often said. The "office" was bare except for a desk, one chair, a narrow cot, a typewriter, and a hook on which Sid placed the black top hat worn by David Niven, playing Phineas Fogg, in *Around the World in Eighty Days*. Here he would stay for long hours of disciplined work.

A paradox of Perelman's life was that both city and country deeply nourished him. He drew great strength from wandering through the streets of any city, but especially New York, London and Dublin. Dublin was a special place for him as the locale of his favorite book, Joyce's *Ulysses*. He knew that city well, but he knew London perhaps even better, with its theaters, parks, alleys and byways.

As for country life, I often visited Sid and Laura in their charming old stone farmhouse in Erwinna, Pa. Sid and Laura bought their house in the depths of the Depression for a couple of thousand dollars, and converted an old chicken house near the main house into an isolated work spot. Sid, who loved nature in its broad aspects, but was somewhat untutored in details, loved to tramp across the fields with Laura and his two children, Adam and Abby, or along a nearby tow canal.

SID had a strong mystical side, an extrasensory area that totally belied his apparently pragmatic approach to life and letters. I recall a Saturday evening many years ago in Erwinna, seated by the big fireplace in the living room, surrounded by shelves filled with what seemed like thousands of books. It was a crisp fall evening, the sort of evening when Sid might decide to tell a particularly hair-raising ghost story. But this evening he called for a Ouija board.

I gave a short laugh, thinking it was some sort of joke. Sid cut me off with a severe look. "I take the Ouija board very seriously," he said. "A few months ago I visited friends in the Adirondacks, and we got out the board and tried to reach Robert Benchley. But they didn't take the board seriously. Thanks to the noise and the laughter, I never reached Benchley, and I had some questions to put to him, especially about humor. Tonight I want to reach Harold Ross [*The New Yorker's* first editor]. I want to ask Ross the same questions."

Sid asked me to place my hands on the board. Nobody made

a sound. We sat a long time, but nothing happened. I felt somewhat embarrassed—and he seemed enormously disappointed.

Not long after he died, I met a devoted old friend of his, who said she had been privileged to catch a peek into a secret corner of his life. "My story is a simple one," she said to me. "It happened after I ran across Sid in London one night after Laura had died."

They had a quiet dinner and walked through Chelsea, heading for the Thames. He reminisced about a book that had made a huge impression upon him when he read it in his teens—*Limehouse Nights* by Thomas Burke. He could still clearly remember the opening lines: "It is a tale of love and lovers that they tell in the low-lit Causeway that slinks from West India Dock Road to the dark waste of waters beyond."

He told her that he had walked down this same dark and dingy street shortly after Laura had died, feeling intensely despondent. He pointed to a dilapidated house and said that he had visited a fortune teller there. Sid had told him that he wanted to discern the future, but the man said he could only talk about the past. He told Sid that he had recently sustained a great loss—perhaps it was his wife—and that it weighed heavily on him. He added that he felt that Sid was a writer, "a considerable writer." Sid again asked about the future. The man told him to return another night.

My friend said that with the fog rolling in from his beloved Thames and half covering his face, the great humorist looked quite desolate and alone. "I never went back," he told my friend. And he never did.

Double Word Power Test No. 6

The Majestic, Elegant Adjective

By PETER FUNK

In this list of adjectives with the suffix *-ic* or *-ant*, check the word or phrase you believe is *nearest in meaning* to the key word. Answers appear at the end of this test.

1. **embryonic** (em brĭ on′ ik)—A: bloated. B: undeveloped. C: fertile. D: dwarfed.
2. **extant** (eks′ tant)—A: prolonged. B: still existing. C: far-reaching. D: inactive.
3. **nostalgic** (nos tal′ jik)—A: indolent. B: diseased. C: homesick. D: soothing.
4. **pliant** (plī′ ant)—A: flexible. B: industrious. C: persistent. D: applicable.
5. **splenetic** (splĕ net′ ik)—A: irritable. B: cutting. C: witty. D: vivacious.
6. **trenchant** (tren′ chant)—A: nimble. B: hearty. C: fleeting. D: incisive.
7. **eulogistic** (ū lo jis′ tik)—A: clairvoyant. B: inflated. C: hopeful. D: laudatory.

8. **resonant** (rez′ ŏ nant)—A: determined. B: logical. C: resounding. D: harsh.

9. **anarchic** (an ar′ kik)—A: despotic. B: lawless. C: outdated. D: corrupt.

10. **vagrant** (vā′ grant)—A: shabby. B: wandering. C: indistinct. D: penniless.

11. **simplistic** (sim plis′ tik)—A: sincere. B: stupid. C: oversimplified. D: clear.

12. **repugnant** (re pug′ nant)—A: homely. B: impudent. C: brutal. D: abhorrent.

13. **archaic** (ar kā′ ik)—A: awkward. B: damaged. C: antiquated. D: original.

14. **piquant** (pē′ kant)—A: irritating. B: comical. C: arch. D: puckish.

15. **euphoric** (ū for′ ik)—A: vague. B. elated. C: forgetful. D: enthusiastic.

16. **rampant** (ram′ pant)—A: unchecked. B: savage. C: confused. D: swollen.

17. **ironic** (ī ron′ ik)—A: inflexible. B: bitter. C: good-natured. D: disguisedly sarcastic.

18. **protuberant** (prō tū′ ber ant)—A: conceited. B: bulging. C: intrusive. D: gushing.

19. **axiomatic** (ak sĭ o mat′ ik)—A: orderly. B: pointed. C: self-evident. D: accurate.

20. **dissonant** (dis′ ŏ nant)—A: stubborn. B: shy. C: discordant. D: muffled.

21. **misanthropic** (mis an throp′ ik)—A: stingy. B: hating mankind. C: heretical. D: depraved.

22. **recalcitrant** (re kal′ sĭ trant)—A: capricious. B: withdrawn. C: aggressive. D: unruly.

23. **acoustic** (a kōōs′ tik)—A: relating to sound. B: corrosive. C: scrambled. D: keen.

24. **sibilant** (sib′ ĭ lant)—A: hissing. B: soft. C: talkative. D: secret.

25. **static** (stăt′ ĭk)—A: inactive. B: leisurely. C: positive. D: confusing.

26. **petulant** (pet′ ū lant)—A: gloomy. B: trivial. C: grudging. D: peevish.

27. **aromatic** (ar o mat′ ik)—A: fragrant. B: crippled. C: sentimental. D: acrid.

28. **tolerant** (tol′ er ant)—A: easygoing. B: forbearing. C: weak. D: unassertive.

29. **laconic** (la kon′ ik)—A: mournful. B: deficient. C: relaxed. D: terse.
30. **flamboyant** (flam boy′ ant)—A: picturesque. B: exaggerated. C: showy. D: deceptive.
31. **apathetic** (ap ǎ thet′ ik)—A: merciless. B: without feeling. C: grudging. D: unyielding.
32. **incessant** (in ses′ ant)—A: unceasing. B: halting. C: oppressive. D: growing.
33. **vitriolic** (vit rǐ ol′ ik)—A: sticky. B: chilling. C: greasy. D: sharp and biting.
34. **cognizant** (kog′ nǐ zant)—A: puzzled. B: aware. C: convinced. D: suspicious.
35. **miasmic** (mī az′ mik)—A: noxious. B: muddy. C: dank. D: pessimistic.
36. **errant** (ěr′ ant)—A: eccentric. B: bold. C: unreliable. D: roving.
37. **spasmodic** (spaz mod′ ik)—A: fitful. B: constant. C: clumsy. D: repeated.
38. **adamant** (ad′ a mant)—A: crystal clear. B: blue. C: unyielding. D: jewel-like.
39. **choleric** (kǒ ler′ ik)—A: feverish. B: pain-racked. C: yellowish. D: hot-tempered.
40. **vibrant** (vī′ brant)—A: full of vigor. B: beautiful. C: wholesome. D: poised.

ANSWERS

1. **embryonic**—B: Undeveloped; beginning; rudimentary; as, an *embryonic* plan. Greek *embryon* (to swell).
2. **extant**—B: Still existing and known; not destroyed or lost; as, the last *extant* member of the species. Latin *exstare* (to be still in existence).
3. **nostalgic**—C: Homesick; eliciting feelings of wistful yearning for a former place or time; as, the *nostalgic* smell of wood smoke. Greek *nostos* (return home) and *algos* (pain).
4. **pliant**—A: Flexible; yielding easily to influence; adaptable; as, a *pliant* nature. Middle French *plier* (to bend, ply).
5. **splenetic**—A: Irritable; peevish; spiteful; as, a *splenetic* outburst. Green *splēn* (spleen), the organ once believed to be the seat of the emotions.

6. **trenchant**—D: Incisive; penetrating; keenly perceptive; as, a *trenchant* argument. Middle French *trenchier* (to cut).

7. **eulogistic**—D: Laudatory; expressing high praise; as, a *eulogistic* book review. Greek *eulogia* (praise).

8. **resonant**—C: Resounding; echoing; full or loud in sound; as, *resonant* tones. Latin *resonare* (to resound).

9. **anarchic**—B: Lawless; relating to a state of political disorder due to the absence of governmental authority; as, an *anarchic* colony. Greek *anarchos* (rulerless).

10. **vagrant**—B: Wandering idly; lacking aim or fixed course; random; as, *vagrant* thoughts. Middle English *vagraunt*.

11. **simplistic**—C: Oversimplified; falsely simple; as, a *simplistic* analysis. French *simplisme* (faulty reasoning, overlooking necessary elements).

12. **repugnant**—D: Abhorrent; arousing extreme dislike or loathing; as, attitudes *repugnant* to our concept of public morality. Latin *repugnare* (to fight against).

13. **archaic**—C: Antiquated; belonging to an earlier period; as, *archaic* thinking. Greek *archaios* (ancient).

14. **piquant**—C: Charmingly arch; intriguing; provocative; as, a *piquant* expression; also, pungent; stimulating to the palate; as, a *piquant* flavor. Middle French *piquer* (to prick, sting).

15. **euphoric**—B: Having a sense of elation, buoyancy, well being, often without discernible cause; as, *euphoric* self-confidence. Greek *euphoros* (healthy).

16. **rampant**—A: Unchecked; unrestrained; flourishing; as, *rampant* growth. Old French *ramper* (to crawl, rear).

17. **ironic**—D: Disguisedly sarcastic; expressing something quite opposite from the literal meaning of the words used; as, a master of *ironic* humor. Greek *eirōn* (dissembler).

18. **protuberant**—B: Bulging; prominent; protruding; as, *protuberant* eyes. Latin *protuberare* (to bulge out).

19. **axiomatic**—C: Self-evident; needing no proof; as, an *axiomatic* truth. Greek *axiōma* (honor).

20. **dissonant**—C: Discordant; inharmonious; lacking agreement; as, *dissonant* voices. Latin *dissonare* (to be discordant).

21. **misanthropic**—B: Marked by hatred or contempt for mankind; as, a *misanthropic* recluse. Greek *misanthrōpos* (hating mankind).

22. **recalcitrant**—D: Unruly; disobedient; difficult to handle

or manage; as, a *recalcitrant* child. Latin *recalcitrare* (to kick back).

23. **acoustic**—A: Relating to sound or hearing; as the *acoustic* problems of a theater. Greek *akouein* (to hear).

24. **sibilant**—A: Hissing; making a hissing sound, like that of the letter *s;* as, the snake's *sibilant* warning. Latin *sibilare* (to hiss, whistle).

25. **static**—A: Inactive; at rest; showing little or no change; dormant; as, the dangers of a *static* foreign policy. Greek *statikos* (causing to stand).

26. **petulant**—D: Peevish; irritable; quick to be annoyed by trifling matters; as, a *petulant* disposition. Latin *petulans* (impudent).

27. **aromatic**—A: Fragrant; having a strong and usually agreeable odor; as, an *aromatic* herb. Greek *arōma* (spice).

28. **tolerant**—B: Forbearing; indulgent; permissive; willing to bear or endure; as, to be *tolerant* of others' faults. Latin *tolerare* (to endure, put up with).

29. **laconic**—D: Terse; sparing of words in speech and writing; concise; as, a *laconic* reply. Greek *Lakōn*, people of a region of ancient Greece who were noted for brevity of speech.

30. **flamboyant**—C: Showy; extravagantly ornate; florid; as, a *flamboyant* costume. French *flamboyer* (to flame).

31. **apathetic**—B: Without feeling or emotion; lacking concern; indifferent; as, an *apathetic* electorate. Greek *apathēs* (without feeling).

32. **incessant**—A: Unceasing; continuing without interruption; as, an incessant talker. Latin incessans, from *in-* (not), and *cessare* (to cease, delay).

33. **vitriolic**—D: Sharp and biting; caustic; virulent; as, a *vitriolic* attack on the nominee. Latin *vitrum* (glass).

34. **cognizant**—B: Aware; conscious; taking heed or notice; as, to be *cognizant* of one's responsibilities. Latin *cognoscere* (to know).

35. **miasmic**—A: Noxious; foul; relating to, caused by or producing a heavy vaporous contamination of the air; as, a *miasmic* blanket of smog. Greek *miasma* (defilement).

36. **errant**—D: Roving; straying out of bounds; deviating from accepted behavior; as, an *errant* youth. Middle French *errer* (to travel).

37. **spasmodic**—A: Fitful; intermittent, acting by fits and starts; as, *spasmodic* efforts to study. Latin *spasmodicus* (marked by twitches).

38. **adamant**—C: Unyielding; unshakable; immovable in opposition; as, an *adamant* stand against detractors. Greek *adamas* (hardest metal, diamond).

39. **choleric**—D: Hot-tempered; fiery; easily moved to anger; irascible; as, a *choleric* disposition. Greek *cholē* (bile)—an excess of which was believed to cause a bad temper.

40. **vibrant**—A: Full of vigor; pulsating with life or activity; responsive; as, a *vibrant* personality. Latin *vibrare* (to vibrate).

VOCABULARY RATINGS

40—36 correct ....master (exceptional)
35—26 correct .... player (excellent)
25—18 correct ....novice (good)

Last Writes

In which tombstone inscriptions from the past mark one's
final jesting place

By GYLES BRANDRETH

Beneath this stone,
the lump of clay,
lies Uncle Peter
Daniels,
Who too early in the month of
May
Took off his winter flannels.

MEDWAY, MASS.

Here lies
Lester Moore
Four slugs
from a .44,
no Les.
no more

TOMBSTONE, ARIZ.

Here lie the bones of Richard Lawton
Whose death, alas! was strangely brought on.
Trying his corns one day to mow off,
His razor slipped and cut his toe off,
His toe, or rather what it grew to,
An inflammation quickly flew to.
Which took, alas! to mortifying,
And was the cause of Richard's dying.

MORETON-IN-MARSH, GLOUCESTERSHIRE

Ruth S. Kibbe, wife
of Alvin J. Stanton
May 5, 1861
Apr 5, 1904
The Lord don't make any mistakes.

SOUTH PLYMOUTH, N.Y.

Beneath this stone, a lump of clay
Lies Arabella Young
Who on the 21st of May
Began to hold her tongue.

HATFIELD, MASS.

Sacred to the memory of
Elisha Philbrook and his wife Sarah.
Beneath these stones do lie,
Back to back, my wife and I!
When the last trumpet the air shall fill,
If she gets up, I'll just lie still.

SARGENTVILLE, MAINE

Here lies the body of our Anna
Done to death by a banana.
It wasn't the fruit that laid her low
But the skin of the thing that made her go.

ENOSBURG, VT.

Played five aces,
Now playing the harp.

DODGE CITY, KAN.

He called Bill Smith a liar.

CRIPPLE CREEK, COLO.

Sacred to the memory of
Jared Bates
who died Aug. the 6th 1800.
His widow, aged 24, lives at 7 Elm
Street, has every
qualification for a
good wife, and yearns
to be comforted.

LINCOLN, MAINE

Underneath this pile of stones
Lies all that's left of Sally Jones.
Her name was Briggs, it was not Jones,
But Jones was used to rhyme with stones.

SKANEATELES, N.Y.

Here lies the body of Mary Ann Lowder
Who burst while drinking a Seidlitz powder
Called from this world to her Heavenly Rest
She should have waited till it effervesced.

BURLINGTON, N.J.

In memory of
Mrs. Alpha White
Weight 309 lbs.
Open wide ye heavenly gates
That lead to the heavenly shore;
Our father suffered in passing through
And mother weighs much more.

LEE, MASS.

Sacred to the memory of inesti-
mable worth of unrivalled excel-
lence and virtue. N.R., whose
ethereal parts became seraphic.
May 25th, 1767.

LITCHFIELD, CONN.

Here lies Jane Smith,
wife of Thomas Smith,
marble cutter. This
monument was erected by
her husband as a
tribute to her memory
and a specimen of his work.
Monuments of the same style 350 dollars.

SPRINGDALE, OHIO

Double Word Power Test No. 7

The Force Be With You

By PETER FUNK

"How forcible are right words," said the prophet Job. There are other ways of gaining power, but none so quick as by adding to your word supply. Test your word power by checking the word or phrase you think is *nearest in meaning* to the key word. Answers appear after this test.

1. **impious** (im′ pĭ us)—A: mischievous. B: irreverent. C: shrewd. D: holy.
2. **tenet** (ten′ et)—A: net. B: resident or dweller. C: opinion held as true. D: experiment.
3. **opprobrious** (ŏ prō′ brĭ us)—A: regarded as worthy. B: shameful. C: opposite. D: angry.
4. **occidental** (ok sĭ den′ t′l)—A: belonging to the West. B: by chance. C: dark and shadowy. D: belonging to the East.
5. **orison** (or′ ĭ zŭn)—A: sacramental cup. B: prayer. C: decoration. D: song.
6. **libido** (lĭ bē′ dō)—A: drunkenness. B: sensual desire. C: freedom. D: something forbidden.

7. **category** (cat′ uh go rē)—A: positive statement. B: impassioned speech. C: division or class. D: thorough questioning.

8. **solace** (sŏl′ iss)—A: peace. B: consolation. C: quiet. D: health.

9. **proscription** (pro scrip′ shun)—A: repeal. B: compulsory enrollment of men. C: physician's formula. D: imposed restriction.

10. **exact** (eg zakt′)—A: to perform correctly. B: keep securely. C: criticize freely. D: demand by authority.

11. **habitat** (hab′ ĭ tat)—A: appearance. B: dress or other outer garment. C: region where something normally lives. D: saddle.

12. **mentor** (men′ tur)—A: old man. B: experienced counselor. C: officer of the law. D: scholar.

13. **vassal** (vass′ uhl)—A: old-time ship. B: container. C: slave. D: Saxon lord.

14. **nuance** (nū′ ahnce; nū ahnce′)—A: hint. B: subtle difference in meaning. C: trickery. D: modesty.

15. **convene** (con vēn′)—A: to make easy. B: call together. C: talk secretly. D: persuade.

16. **carousel** (kar o sel′; kar ōō sel′)—A: merry-go-round. B: chime. C: wild drinking party. D: whirling dance.

17. **morass** (mo rass′)—A: marsh. B: confusion. C: melancholy. D: abyss.

18. **imposture** (im poss′ chŏor)—A: heavy burden. B: stooping position. C: fraud or trickery to gain an end. D: handicap.

19. **foray** (for′ ā)—A: tropical fish. B: raid. C: display. D: failure.

20. **asseverate** (ă sev′ er āt)—A: to state emphatically. B: be proud. C: cut in two. D: annoy or irritate.

21. **fitful** (fit′ ful)—A: nervous. B: demented. C: restless. D: mean.

22. **arrogant** (ar′ o gant)—A: diffident. B: quarrelsome. C: confirmed. D: haughty.

23. **curator** (kū rā′ ter)—A: administrator. B: assistant priest. C: devotee of the arts. D: physician.

24. **sanction** (sank′ shun)—A: to nullify. B: consecrate. C: approve. D: warn.

25. **viscid** (vĭs′ ĭd)—A: persistent. B: burning. C: innermost. D: sticky.

26. **mercenary** (mer′ se ner ē)—A: scheming. B: greedy. C: disloyal. D: fickle.

27. **traverse** (tra vurs'; trav' ers)—A: to mark off. B: split. C: cross. D: backtrack.

28. **auxiliary** (og zil' ya rē)—A: helpful. B: subsequent. C: superfluous. D: essential.

29. **blasphemy** (blas' fe mē)—A: malicious charge. B: rebellion. C: violent outburst. D: irreverence.

30. **gaudy** (gaw' dē)—A: tricky. B: brash. C: flashy. D: coarse.

31. **excerpt** (ek surpt'; ek'-)—A: to erase. B: abridge. C: extract. D: adapt.

32. **condolence** (kon dō' lens; kon'-)—A: permission. B: sympathy. C: forgiveness. D: sloth.

33. **unkempt** (un kempt')—A: disheveled. B: coarse. C: rattled. D: free.

34. **placid** (plas' id)—A: dull. B: motionless. C: limp. D: calm.

35. **mannerism** (man' er iz'm)—A: polite behavior. B: eccentricity. C: attitude. D: shortcoming.

36. **hapless** (hap' les)—A: forlorn. B: sad. C: feeble. D: unfortunate.

37. **verdant** (ver' dant)—A: lively. B: excessively wordy. C: green. D: wandering.

38. **stolid** (stŏl' id)—A: sturdy. B: stubborn. C: reliable. D: impassive.

39. **impolitic** (im pol' ĭ tik)—A: unwise. B: bipartisan. C: unregenerate. D: detached.

40. **unscathed** (un skāthed')—A: smooth. B: unharmed. C: empty. D: relaxed.

ANSWERS

1. **impious**—B: Irreverent; lacking in respect; profane; wicked; as, "He lived a life that was pagan and *impious*." Latin *impius* from *im-* (not) and *pius* (reverent).

2. **tenet**—C: An opinion, principle or doctrine held as true; as, "The *tenet* of the totalitarian is that men must be guided and controlled." Latin *tenere* (to hold).

3. **opprobrious**—B: Shameful; odious; disgraceful. Latin *ob-* (upon) and *probrum* (disgrace).

4. **occidental**—A: From a Latin word meaning "to set, as the sun," and applied by Asian countries to the lands west of them. Hence, of or belonging to the West.

5. **orison**—B: Prayer; words appropriate to prayer; as, "The monks were heard chanting their *orisons*." Latin *orare* (to pray).

6. **libido**—B: In both Latin and English this means sensual desire; violent longing; emotional craving; a primal urge; as, "They tried to sublimate their *libido* in religious devotion."

7. **category**—C: Division or class; as, "Today's taxes fall into three major *categories*."

8. **solace**—B: Originally from Latin *solor*, meaning consolation; comfort in grief or calamity; as, "Keeping busy has brought *solace* to millions of souls."

9. **proscription**—D: An imposed restriction or restraint; as, "The dictator issued a *proscription* of all civil rights."

10. **exact**—D: To demand by authority; to levy or extort; as, "Kidnapers usually *exact* ransom."

11. **habitat**—C: A region where something normally lives or is found; as, "The Rockies are the *habitat* of the mountain lion." Latin *habitatio* (dwelling).

12. **mentor**—B: In the *Odyssey*, Ulysses has left his son's education to Mentor, an old and trusted friend. Thus the word has come to mean a wise and experienced counselor.

13. **vassal**—C: Originally one who held land under a superior lord. Hence, a slave; as, "Hitler virtually reduced his countrymen to *vassals*." Medieval Latin *vassallus* (servant).

14. **nuance**—B: A French loan-word that means a slight difference in shading or coloration. Hence, a subtle difference in anything perceptible to the mind; as, "His tone of voice gave an unfriendly *nuance* to an otherwise friendly word."

15. **convene**—B: Call together; convoke; summon to assemble; as, "The President will *convene* a special session of Congress." Latin *con-* (together) and *venire* (to come).

16. **carousel**—A: Once this meant a military tournament or pageant; but now the word, of Italian inheritance, applies to the ordinary amusement-park merry-go-round.

17. **morass**—A: A marsh, swamp or quagmire; hence, any distressing difficulty hard to get out of. Dutch *moeras*.

18. **imposture**—C: Fraud or trickery to gain an end; deception. Originally from the Latin *in* (on) and *ponere* (to place).

19. **foray**—B: Raiding expedition; as, "The enemy made a dawn *foray*." Old French *forrer* (to pillage).

20. **asseverate**—A: To state emphatically; affirm solemnly;

make an earnest and positive declaration. Latin *asseverare* (to act with earnestness).

21. **fitful**—C: Restless; spasmodic; intermittent; irregular; as *fitful* sleep. Old English *fitt* (strife) and *-ful*.

22. **arrogant**—D: Haughty; overbearing; offensively demanding; as, an *arrogant* official. Latin *arrogare* (to claim, assume).

23. **curator**—A: Administrator, especially one in charge of all or part of a museum, zoo or similar place of exhibit; as, *curator* of Indian artifacts. Latin *curare* (to care for).

24. **sanction**—C: To approve officially; ratify; confirm; as, to *sanction* a new law. Latin *sancire* (to make holy).

25. **viscid**—D: Sticky; adhesive; having gluelike texture; as, an unpleasant *viscid* surface. Latin *viscidus*, from *viscum* (birdlime).

26. **mercenary**—B: Greedy; motivated by money; venal; as, a *mercenary* concern over gate receipts. Latin *mercenarius*, from *merces* (wages).

27. **traverse**—C: To cross; travel over; cross and recross; as, to *traverse* a steep slope. Latin *transvertere* (to turn across).

28. **auxiliary**—A: Helpful; supplementary; giving additional support; reserve; as, a sailboat's *auxiliary* engine. Latin *auxilium* (help).

29. **blasphemy**—D: Irreverence toward God or things held sacred or inviolable; profanation; as, a breach of historical precedent amounting to *blasphemy*. Greek *blasphēmos* (evil-speaking).

30. **gaudy**—C: Flashy; tastelessly showy; as, a *gaudy* costume. Middle English *gaude*.

31. **excerpt**—C: To extract; choose or select for quotation; as, to *excerpt* a passage from Shakespeare. Latin *excerpere* (to pick out).

32. **condolence**—B: Sympathy with another in sorrow; commiseration; consolation; as, a letter of *condolence*. Latin *condolescere* (to suffer).

33. **unkempt**—A: Disheveled; untidy; lacking order and trimness; as, an *unkempt* garden. Middle English *un-* (not) and *kemben* (to comb).

34. **placid**—D: Calm; complacent; undisturbed; as, a *placid* disposition. Latin *placidus* (quiet, still, gentle).

35. **mannerism**—B: Eccentricity; habitual peculiarity of action, bearing or expression; as, a disconcerting *mannerism* of

speech. Old French *maniere* (way of acting) and *-ism*.

36. **hapless**—D: Unfortunate; unlucky; as, the *hapless* flood victims. Old Norse *happ* (good luck) and Old English *-lēas* (devoid of).

37. **verdant**—C: Green with vegetation; lush; as, *verdant* fields; also, unripe in experience or judgment; unsophisticated; raw; as, *verdant* youth. Latin *viridis* (green).

38. **stolid**—D: Impassive; unemotional; not easily excited or moved; as, a *stolid* judge. Latin *stolidus* (unmovable).

39. **impolitic**—A: Unwise; not expedient or prudent; as, an untimely and *impolitic* disclosure. *In-* (not) and Greek *politikos* (political).

40. **unscathed**—B: Unharmed; not injured; as, to emerge from combat *unscathed*. Middle English *un-* (not) and *scathen* (to scathe, injure).

VOCABULARY RATINGS

40—36 correct .... master (exceptional)
35—26 correct .... player (excellent)
25—18 correct .... novice (good)

Scramblish, in One Easy Lesson

By CHRISTOPHER LUCAS

I've been promised a *flash* toilet in Pakistan, and I've eaten steamed *muscles* in Nagasaki. In Taiwan, I've marveled at a tailor's sign that vowed: "Ladies can have fits here," and fumbled through an Italian mail-order catalogue that threatened clients with "a speedy execution."

I know a Spanish car-rental office that boasts "Without competitive prices!" and a Leningrad restaurant that has a cloakroom sign urging, "Please hang yourself here." But then even the British are guilty of disfiguring speech. Consider this ad from a small-town newspaper: "Children shot for Christmas in the home. Call Regent Studios."

What *are* they doing to the English language? The preceding are examples of a linguistic wave that has splashed across the world. Modern English has become the most popular language in history. In addition to the more than 300 million people who speak it as a mother tongue, a *billion* or so use some kind of English as a second language. In this swirling, seething Babel, it's only natural that curious things occur. Words corkscrew wildly, spelling runs amok, meanings turn inside out, grammar takes a holiday. Call it broken, mangled, fractured, clobbered or just plain scrambled English—or, for short, Scramblish. It's a language that can be both entertaining and utterly misleading, poetic and meaningless, inspired and lunatic.

Over the years I've roamed some five dozen countries and collected choice samples of Scramblish. I've discovered its varieties on every continent. Whether it's called Japlish, Franglais or pidgin-English, Scramblish, the poor man's Esperanto, knows no frontiers.

Who wouldn't be seduced by this masterly invitation to a shark-fishing trip in Tahiti? "Choice the best," sings the brochure. "Goo fortt ou Board m/y The shark fissing boat. Leef the harbor at 10am an have your fan, on board. A luxury 21m fissing boat, folly equiped for navigation. Roods reels baits and tution by a very experimentd crew. Return at 4pm afther 6 hours of fan sun chaine relax and adventure." What a day!

In Italy, I saw this placard on a church door: "Beware! Falling Angels!" (They meant statues, not seraphim.) And the following street sign in Java: "Attention! You must be well dressed on the road. Violating this rule you will be seized and confiscated."

Around the world, restaurants are particularly inspired. I have ordered "breded fillet pork catlet" in Penang, "rare cheese-cake" in Nagoya, and a "Grilled Chinese and Ham on Toast" in Hong Kong. "Eat the Middle East foods in an European ambulance," offered a Teheran steakhouse.

Hotel notices boast some of the finest Scramblish available. One well-meaning Tokyo hotel warns, "Swindlers dangling with guests around our hotel at night have no relations with us." And how about this for inscrutability: "Elevator repaired. This elevator cannot be used."

The world's different forms of pidgin-English have created whole new idioms. Scramblish, yes, but high-level stuff. In Macao, I reveled in such phrases as: "You topside box no savvy" (Your brain does not comprehend) and "That fella completely sick" (He's dead). But no other pidgin has the evocative power and imagination of Tok Pisin, Papua New Guinea's lingua franca. Just savor the vocabulary: *antap* (on top) means "above"; *samting nogul* (something no good) is "evil." The inventive Papua New Guineans have even tackled Shakespeare:

Pren, man belong Rom, wantok, harim nau ("Friends, Romans, countrymen, lend me your ears"). Yu laikim? The greatest.

Ultimately, the sneakiest examples of Scramblish lull the victim into thinking he's actually reading English; then *wham!*—he's up to his eyeballs in verbal quicksand. A brochure to France's Basque coast opens innocently enough: "Those who visit the area will not find great historical monuments, majestic architecture or memories of events from a sensational past." Then: "The Basque coast is more importance than the inland parts, and therefore more visitores and sperdy time over. It has charm of its oun, wild, with the mountains nearing the sea, and the waves foamines on the rocks like wild horses, with manes flowires." Sheer poetry! Kelley or Sheats, maybe.

Triple Test

Super Word Power Quiz

By PETER FUNK

The 60 quiz words here are ranked on three plateaus of difficulty—Novice, Player and Master. All the words have been selected from articles and excerpts in The Digest. Select the definition you think is correct. Answers appear after this test.

1. **orbit**—A: path of a heavenly body. B: enclosure. C: plant. D: cloud.
2. **limber**—A: synchronized. B: unbending. C: easy going. D: flexible.
3. **abolish**—A: to put an end to. B: hide away. C: make shine. D: be mistaken.
4. **treacherous**—A: very steep. B: not to be trusted. C: pulled apart. D: shallow.
5. **microscopic** (mī kruh skop′ ik)—A: stringy. B: rather large. C: colorful. D: extremely small.
6. **foster**—A: to help to develop. B: manufacture. C: settle down. D: explore.

7. **flicker**—A: strike quickly. B: sweep. C: react. D: burn unsteadily or waver.

8. **hamper**—A: to put away. B: launder. C: call off. D: interfere with.

9. **germane**—(jer mān′)—A: growing. B: relevant. C: disciplined. D: essential.

10. **yoke**—A: horse paddock. B: strong rope. C: funny story. D: wooden harness.

11. **majestic**—A: religious. B: unusual. C: tall. D: stately and dignified.

12. **submerge**—A: to walk on. B: join. C: spread. D: put under water.

13. **legendary** (lej′ un der ē)—having to do with A: fashions. B: weights and measures. C: myths and folk tales. D: untruths.

14. **straggler**—someone who A: grows angry. B: acts lazy. C: falls behind. D: looks untidy.

15. **significance**—A: hint. B: puzzle. C: autograph. D: meaning.

16. **heredity**—A: inherited characteristics. B: traditional clothes. C: argument. D: ceremony.

17. **descent** (dē sent′)—A: downward slope. B: disagreement. C: cavern. D: coin.

18. **novelty**—A: short story. B: antique. C: beginner. D: something new or unusual.

19. **aspect**—A: focal point. B: look or appearance. C: rumor. D: clarity.

20. **sparse**—A: thinly scattered. B: very stingy. C: closemouthed. D: flat.

21. **relish**—A: to celebrate. B: enjoy. C: prosper. D: yearn for.

22. **harbor**—A: to be enthusiastic about. B: reinforce. C: keep under control. D: hold in mind.

23. **fulcrum**—A: lever's support point. B: windlass or winch. C: block and tackle. D: engine block.

24. **plight**—A: quick retreat. B: pleasing suggestion. C: an infestation. D: difficult situation.

25. **prank**—A: fantasy. B: folk dance. C: stinging remark. D: joke or trick.

26. **proton**—A: sunspot. B: part of atom's nucleus. C: nerve connection. D: food element.

27. **collage** (kuh lazh′)—A: a shading. B: university. C: chorus. D: art form.

28. **affiliate** (uh fil′ ē ate)—A: to effect. B: trust. C: attract. D: join.

29. **profound**—A: superfluous. B: biased. C: devout. D: deep or complete.

30. **transitory**—A: imperfect. B: durable. C: temporary. D: filmy.

31. **scope**—A: agenda. B: patriarch. C: range, area or extent. D: educated guess.

32. **caste**—A: form or mold. B: fishing tactic. C: acting troupe. D: social class.

33. **zenith**—A: highest point. B: horizon. C: lowest place. D: objective.

34. **subsidy**—A: financial aid. B: act of undermining. C: framework. D: abatement.

35. **inviolable** (in vī′ o la b′l)—A: honorable. B: unassailable. C: illegal. D: unworkable.

36. **pungent**—A: very clever. B: acrid or sharp. C: obtuse or dull. D: unpleasant or disagreeable.

37. **obliterate** (ub blit′ uh rāt)—A: to blot out. B: smooth over. C: go away from. D: disapprove of.

38. **psyche** (sī′ kē)—A: Indian holy man. B: occult power. C: emotional distress. D: human soul or mind.

39. **insuperable** (in soo puh ruh b′l)—A: unbearable. B: ineffable. C: insurmountable. D: intolerable.

40. **context**—A: competitive game. B: surrounding words or circumstances. C: fact or statistic. D: bounds of an area.

41. **feint**—A: to be mislead by a false move. B: dare or defy. C: take away or remove. D: lose consciousness.

42. **nuzzle**—A: to silence. B: spray. C: kiss softly. D: rub gently with the nose.

43. **eclectic**—A: concise. B: full. C: choosing from various sources. D: rife.

44. **pariah**—A: Hindu ruler. B: an outcast. C: head of family. D: vehicle.

45. **detriment** (det′ ruh ment)—A: dislike. B: resolve. C: harm. D: remainder.

46. **unassuming**—A: modest. B: irresponsible. C: satisfied. D: unimportant.

47. **convivial** (kun viv′ ē ul)—A: witty. B: noisy. C: energetic. D: sociable.

48. **maelstrom** (māl′ strum)—A: heavy rainstorm. B: large whirlpool. C: great wickedness. D: severe criticism.

49. **eclipse**—A: to outshine. B: fasten. C: cut out. D: silhouette.

50. **wane**—A: to burgeon. B: disappear. C: decrease. D: blanch.
51. **iconoclast** one who—A: retires from the world. B: is an individualist. C: is an idealist. D: attacks traditional beliefs.
52. **guileless** (gīl′ les)—A: innocent. B: weak. C: modest. D: languid.
53. **ambuscade**—A: an ambush. B: mask. C: reveler. D: covering.
54. **maw**—A: unpleasant taste. B: building's foundation. C: animal's throat or stomach. D: type of hydraulic hammer.
55. **ineffable** (in ef′ uh b′l)—A: not erasable. B: inadequate. C: inexpressible. D: not effective.
56. **ken**—A: knowledge. B: relatives. C: symbolism. D: viewpoint.
57. **legerdemain** (lej ur duh main′)—A: sleight of hand. B: nonsense. C: thoughtless boasting. D: story telling.
58. **meretricious**—A: falsely charming. B: excessively prideful. C: especially obnoxious. D: praiseworthy.
59. **simulacrum** (sim yoo lay′ crum)—A: image or likeness. B: miniature vase. C: monumental tomb. D: measuring instrument.
60. **velodrome** (vě′ luh drome)—A: type of staircase. B: arena with a bicycle track. C: furry skin. D: dirigible hanger.

ANSWERS

1.–A	2.–D	3.–A	4.–B
5.–D	6.–A	7.–D	8.–D
9.–B	10.–D	11.–D	12.–D
13.–C	14.–C	15.–D	16.–A
17.–A	18.–D	19.–B	20.–A
21.–B	22.–D	23.–A	24.–D
25.–D	26.–B	27.–D	28.–D
29.–D	30.–C	31.–C	32.–D
33.–A	34.–A	35.–B	36.–B
37.–A	38.–D	39.–C	40.–B
41.–A	42.–D	43.–C	44.–B
45.–C	46.–A	47.–D	48.–B
49.–A	50.–C	51.–D	52.–A
53.–A	54.–C	55.–C	56.–A
57.–A	58.–A	59.–A	60.–B

VOCABULARY RATINGS

55—60 correct ....master (exceptional)
30—55 correct .... player (excellent)
20—30 correct ...:.........................novice (good)

Words
Are an Adventure

By I. A. R. WYLIE

A few weeks ago I was walking along a bridle path with a friend who has a trick of picking up unconsidered trifles of knowledge. Two riders trotted past and then broke into a canter.

"It's amusing to think where the word 'canter' comes from," my companion remarked. "Most of the pilgrims on their way to Thomas à Becket's tomb at Canterbury traveled on horseback and, I suppose, got rather bored by their sedate progress. To have galloped would have been indecorous, but a sober intermediate gait broke the monotony. So the word 'canter' came into usage. And incidentally the flowers we call Canterbury bells owe their name to the bells which the pilgrims attached to their horses' necks."

My companion went on to the humble dandelion—really an aristocratic Frenchman called *dent de lion*, its little yellow petals reminding someone of a lion's teeth. It's easy to see how *dent de lion* became "dandelion."

Here was a new interest free for the taking. I began tracking down familiar words on my own and soon discovered Wilfred

Funk's book *Word Origins,* from which I have selected a few trophies that may whet your interest.

I had supposed that many of our words were simply modern slang, whereas in fact they are historically respectable. The word "guy," for instance. The original guy was a scoundrel called Guy Fawkes who on the fifth of November, 1605, plotted to blow up the Houses of Parliament. He was caught in the nick of time, tortured and executed. But from that day to this, English children rig up a rag effigy and carry it through the London streets chanting:

> Remember, remember the Fifth of November . . .
> For gunpowder plot shall not be forgot.

The word "slapstick" did not, as one might think, originate with the late Mack Sennett. In the 17th century the English employed a form of entertainment which, to this day, is an essential part of Christmas festivities. It is called pantomime. Two of its chief characters are Harlequin and the Clown. Harlequin is always armed with two laths, loosely bound together so that when they land on the clown's bald pate or any other part of his anatomy they give off a resounding "slap." Hence the slapstick which we have come to associate with broad farce.

All of us eat sandwiches at one time or another without giving a thought to their noble inventor—a certain Earl of Sandwich who was such an inveterate gambler that he refused to take time off from the gambling table to eat a regular meal. In fact we owe the English aristocracy quite a few everyday items. It was the Earl of Cardigan who popularized the style of woolen sweater which he wore during the Crimean War. Another officer in that campaign, Lord Raglan, we have to thank for the raglan sleeve.

Businessmen still "dicker," probably unaware that their activities date back to the early Romans and their purchase of pelts from the barbarians. The Latin for a set of ten was *decuria,* and it became the accepted unit in fur-trade negotiations. By slow process *decuria* became our "dicker."

In the dark ages of our past a man lost at night in the forest would hear sinister rustlings and, imagining that the god Pan was after him, would take to his heels in pan-ic. We speak of lunatics. Our ancestors believed that the moon—*luna*—had an evil influence on men's minds. Under certain circumstances they became "moonstruck."

The stars too played their part in human affairs. When they were adverse, men foresaw "disaster"—*dis* being Latin for "against" and *astrum* meaning "star." But though we use the word "disaster," we no longer credit the stars with our misfortunes, even though we sometimes speak of someone as being ill-starred.

"Bunk" and "debunk" are pure American. In 1820 a tiresome member of the House of Representatives from North Carolina apologized for his windy and irrelevant discourse by explaining that he was really addressing himself to his own constituents in Buncombe County.

We all know how a steeplechase is run, over a prescribed course dotted with fences and ditches and booby traps. But why "steeple"? Well, in the old days young racing bloods would pick out a distant church steeple and ride for it, hell-for-leather, over fields, hedges, brooks and gardens, the shorter and more dangerous the cut the better.

Words are, as Wilfred Funk charmingly describes them, "little windows through which we can look into the past." Even those that time has dimmed or broken deserve our respect and wonder.

Words That Have Appeared in These Tests

MS READ-a-thon—
a simple way to start youngsters reading

Boys and girls between 6 and 14 can join the MS READ-a-thon and help find a cure for Multiple Sclerosis by reading books. And they get two rewards — the enjoyment of reading, and the great feeling that comes from helping others.

Parents and educators: For complete information call your local MS chapter. Or mail the coupon below.

Kids can help, too!